The Computer in Composition Instruction

The Computer in Composition Instruction

A Writer's Tool

Edited by

William Wresch
University of Wisconsin Center, Marinette

National Council of Teachers of English
1111 Kenyon Road, Urbana, Illinois 61801

Dedicated to Dean William Schmidtke

Book Design: Tom Kovacs for TGK Design

NCTE Stock Number 08156

Library of Congress Cataloging in Publication Data

The Computer in composition instruction.

    Bibliography: p.
    1. English language—Rhetoric—Study and Teaching—Data processing—Addresses, essays, lectures.   2. English language—Composition and exercises—Study and teaching—Data processing—Addresses, essays, lectures.   3. Computer-assisted instruction—Addresses, essays, lectures.
4. Word processing—Addresses, essays, lectures.
I. Wresch, William, 1947–
PE1404.C63   1984   808′.042′02854   84-16620
ISBN 0-8141-0815-6

Contents

Introduction

William Wresch
University of Wisconsin Center, Marinette

Planning for this book began in the fall of 1981, a time of growing interest in how computers might be used to help teach writing. Where there had been little interest, now every national and regional English teacher's convention had at least a few sessions on computers and some had many. The Conference on College Composition and Communication was especially active, offering numerous computer sessions at both its 1982 and 1983 conventions. Not surprisingly, the profession also began writing about the topic. I published two articles in *College English* (1982, 1983) describing many of the major composition programs. Conduit dedicated an issue of *Pipeline* (vol. 8, Summer 1983) to computers and composition as did *The Writing Instructor* (vol. 2, Summer 1983). At about the same time, the South West Regional Laboratory published a pamphlet describing several approaches to computers and composition (Lawlor 1982).

Given all this activity, English instructors had a variety of sources from which to gain initial information about the educational uses of computers. What they didn't have, however, was a source that described these computer projects in detail and discussed how they were actually conceived and developed. The special journal issues usually had only four or five articles, most of them brief. And convention sessions typically had to observe a 20-minute time limit.

This book was created to solve these problems. First, because it is a book, it can describe more programs than journals and pamphlets, and, in fact, this book examines 13 major projects under way in the United States. More importantly, each project is thoroughly described, including information on program operation, program development, and classroom use.

The last two points—development and use—are important. While the projects described in this book are highly regarded, the use of computers for composition instruction is so new and developing so rapidly that there is no way of knowing for sure if any of the 13 approaches will still be

1

used in five years. Of more long lasting value, then, is the process the program authors used to create their projects and integrate them into the traditional educational process. A record of this process should have long-term value for instructors who either develop their own uses for computers or adopt the programs developed by others.

The book is divided into four parts. The first three chapters describe programs mainly concerned with prewriting. The next three chapters describe editing and grammar programs. These are followed by three chapters concerned with word processor research and applications. The last four chapters focus on the use of programs that integrate the whole writing process. Each chapter is organized in roughly the same way: the reasons for developing the program, program description, the development process, program use, program evaluation, and thoughts for the future. At the end of most chapters, technical specifications and information on program availability are furnished. The organization of the book and the organization of the chapters should allow readers to find easily whatever information they are interested in. To enhance the book's use as a reference, both a glossary of computer terms and an annotated bibliography have been included.

Why Computers and Composition?

A valid question to consider before going any further is, Why the sudden interest in using computers to teach composition? Digital computers have been around nearly 40 years and composition instruction has been around a good deal longer. Each has gotten along quite nicely without the other. Why are so many people now interested in joining the two? One possible answer is that our profession is trying to keep up with the "real world." With Wang word processors in every major office and automated spelling checkers available for as little as $100 and stylistic analyzers like Grammatik advertised in popular magazines, a sense of panic might be expected.

But that doesn't seem to be the major motivation behind the development currently taking place. When asked about their motivation, the authors in this book responded with such answers as "to encourage students to revise and edit more fully," "to study composing on computers," "hoped . . . that word processors with editing software might provide help for declining writing and editing skills," "intrigued by the work of Hugh Burns," "I needed help with my freshman writing courses," and "inspired by the possibilities of Ellen Nold's and Hugh Burns's programs." These are clearly not the comments of people in a race with technology. These are people who are dedicated to teaching writing and who are looking for better methods. Their references to developers of early composition programs make it clear they researched the work already done and saw what they thought were possibilities for teaching students in new and better ways.

What are these ways? Each chapter in this collection begins with a description of advantages authors see in their computer-assisted writing programs, so I won't attempt a detailed analysis here. There is, however, a pattern worth noting. These authors and others who have discussed the subject usually cite six advantages to computerized instruction.

The first is individualized instruction. This may seem ironic to some who still see computers as the first step in turning our students into robots, but for those familiar with computers, the point is well understood. Raymond Rodrigues (Chapter 2) exploits this capability with a program that includes a variety of prewriting activities so students can use what works best for them as individuals. Christine Neuwirth (Chapter 13) even has levels of student aids in her program so that students receive as much or as little information about a writing problem as they need. The result is that unlike a student using a book or workbook, a student using a well-designed program can experience a unique series of activities.

Another feature of most good programs is that they provide help when it is most needed. Every instructor has spent innumerable class hours discussing everything from comma splices to elements of style only to have the lecture fall on deaf ears because students needed the information not while sitting in the class, but later sitting at a desk (or a terminal) doing some writing. Several of the programs described in this collection can teach students what they need to know when they need to know it—that is, when they write—and can often explain an area of writing in terms of the compositions the students are currently drafting.

This timeliness of instruction is enhanced by another ability of some of the newer computer composition programs—feature analysis. Where students have typically had to wait days or even weeks before getting a response to their work from a teacher, the computer can respond to some aspects of their writing in seconds, often while the student is still writing. Whether it be simple spelling checkers or an analysis of style and organization, computer programs can respond to what students have written, giving them a continuing "audience" which in some cases not only comments on text but supplies lessons and possible corrections should a student desire them.

Another advantage, one being mentioned more and more frequently, is effective use of students' time. Here the example generally used is the revision of essays. If a student prepares an essay with pen and pencil or on a typewriter, revising that paper to respond to any teacher comments involves not only rewriting those parts of the essay an instructor has marked for revision, but also transcribing all the sentences in between.

This means much of a student's time is spent in mindless copying. With a computer operating as a word processor, however, a student can jump to those sentences marked by the instructor, fix them, and leave the rest of the essay alone. Revising time is used for genuine revision—not mere transcription.

Some researchers also comment on the way computers help some students see prose as "fluid." Proficient writers are aware that ideas can be presented in different sequences with different emphases, tones, styles, etc. Unfortunately, some students tend to see words on a page as fixed. A word processor can very quickly and easily show these students that words, sentences, even whole paragraphs can be juggled to test for effect. Often it takes only seeing a few sentences move around on the screen for such students to realize, suddenly, that writing is a very dynamic art.

A last commonly cited advantage is freedom to write. Most instructors need try only one freewriting activity to know that many students simply can't generate words in any great quantity. There are many reasons for this, but one seems to be that students get bogged down in checking for spelling, grammar, and punctuation long before they ask themselves if the sentence they are working on so laboriously even belongs in their paper. Computers can help these students by making it easy for them to go back later and correct errors; they can even help them find the errors. This freedom from the immediate need to correct helps many students produce larger quantities of words faster, and enough has been said about the value of pure verbal volume in writing development to make this advantage clear. Of course Ruth Von Blum is quick to point out in Chapter 11 that such volume production may lead some easily satisfied students to substitute quantity for quality, but both she and Kate Kiefer, in Chapter 4, describe how the computer can help with that problem as well.

In summary, the advantages generally listed for computers are individualized instruction, timely assistance and feedback, effective use of student time, a sense of the fluidity of ideas, and a freedom to produce text. Other observers may produce a list of disadvantages just as long, but for a teaching method still in its infancy and subject to rapid change, at least it is clear that computer-assisted composition has potential and warrants the interest it is currently attracting.

The History of Computers and Composition

The first thing a reader may notice about the programs described in this book is that they are all new; in fact, many are still being developed or tested. Even the oldest program described, Hugh Burns's TOPOI, dates back only to 1978. Computer composition programs seemingly appeared out of thin air just a few years ago.

Actually there were a number of attempts to teach English with the help of computers in the mid-1960s, when computer time became inexpensive enough to be used for instruction. The early programs generally utilized the programmed learning model B. F. Skinner (1964) outlines in his article "Why We Need Teaching Machines." The programs taught such concepts as spelling rules, capitalization, punctuation, and grammar by taking students step by step through "frames" in which short lessons were followed by brief tests to determine if students had mastered the spelling or grammar rule taught. Drill and practice programs had many initial adherents who praised the immediate feedback students received from the programs and the fact that some programs were ingeniously arranged to take students logically from concept to concept and could even jump back to certain concepts if it became clear from a student's answers that he or she was confused.

Programs of this type are still available from such sources as PLATO and the Minnesota Educational Computing Consortium. Critics point out that the drills are tenuously related to the writing process and thus may have limited usefulness, while others think the programs may be appropriate for some types of students. Michael Southwell discusses this issue fully in Chapter 6.

Whatever the complaints about or praise for drill and practice programs, the fact is they were used because they were the only aspect of English education computers were capable of teaching. Richard Atkinson (1969) spoke longingly about "dialogue" systems in which the computer would understand and respond to words and ideas of students; but these programs didn't exist, and computers couldn't understand students beyond whether or not they had answered "C" to question 4, "2" to question 5, and "YES" to question 6. That's not much of a dialogue.

The first real work towards programs that would respond to student writing began with Ellis Page of the University of Wisconsin in 1968. He painstakingly punched student essays onto computer cards so that the computers of the day could analyze the essays for sentence length, word length, subordination, coordination, essay length, and many other quantifiable features. By comparing the results of the computer analysis with the evaluations of human graders, Page felt that a correlation could be established between the degree of presence of some features and general quality of the text. If there were a correlation, computers could at least sort out those essays likely to be weak. Repetition of Page's studies seemed to indicate that computers could in fact do this sorting.

A related study by Hiller, Marcotte, and Martin (1969) used the computer to search for the presence of certain vague, "opinionated," or specific words in student essays and correlated the presence or absence of words in these categories with grades human evaluators gave the essays. They too felt the correlation was sufficient for computer discrimination of possibly weak essays. Approaches similar to those described by Page and Hiller have found their way into the new computer editing programs described in this book by Cohen (Chapter 5) and Kiefer (Chapter 4).

Another pioneer is Ellen Nold, who was experimenting with computer uses at Stanford University in the early 1970s. Rather than use the computer to analyze what students had written, she used it to start students thinking. Advanced programming languages were by then available, allowing her to construct programs that asked students questions and partially "understood" their answers. But instead of attempting a dialogue with students, she tried to ask them sufficient questions to help them identify an essay subject, an audience, and an organization for their ideas. Burns, Helen Schwartz, and I all credit Nold with supplying the basis for our work in automated prewriting.

During the 1970s, word processors also became increasingly available. Initially ungainly programs available only for huge computers, they were by the end of the decade much more sophisticated, much less expensive, and available even for inexpensive microcomputers. Colette Daiute (Chapter 9), Lillian Bridwell and Donald Ross (Chapter 7), and Stephen Marcus (Chapter 8) discuss how the availability of such word processors changed writing instruction. Their importance is also reflected in the experimental systems developed by Von Blum (Chapter 11) and Neuwirth (Chapter 13).

Taken together, the analyzer programs of Page and Hiller, the questioner programs of Nold, and the new word processors established the basis for every one of the programs described in this book. Individual developers and users may have chosen to follow Nold rather than Page or have chosen word processors rather than either one, but everyone working in computers and composition has chosen one, two, or all three of them as a starting point for her or his work. Computers in composition *do* have a history.

The Developers

While I have looked briefly at why there is an interest in using computers to teach writing and at the history of that effort, I haven't said too much about the people involved. Who are these people spending so many hours developing computer programs?

First and foremost, they are English teachers. The authors of this collection have anywhere from seven to 19 years of experience teaching

English at the high school and college level. All also have both graduate and undergraduate training in English; each has a Ph.D. in either English or education.

Thus, they are not a group of computer hackers who suddenly decided to start creating programs in writing instruction. As a matter of fact, fully half of the authors have never taken a computer science course, while most of the rest have had only one or two introductory-level courses. Only two authors have had more than two courses in computer programming. These are English teachers who became programmers, not vice versa.

How were they able to produce very complex programs? For most of them, it was just a matter of learning on their own. Introductory courses or books may have helped, but by and large once they decided what they wanted the computer to do, they just kept programming and reprogramming until it did it. Like many others, Rodrigues describes his happy surprise that "computer programming is not an unsolvable mystery." His is the majority opinion. Writing nearly ten years ago about those in our profession who feel computers *are* an unsolvable mystery, Nold (1975, 272–73) said, "It is ironic that a group known to undertake calmly and surely the study of Latin, Greek, Russian, Chinese, Swahili, or Gaelic often balks at the much simpler task of learning the more logical, far less capricious, language of the machine."

Which is not to say that everyone who wishes to produce writing programs needs to learn the language of the machine. A number of projects described in this book were developed through the use of student programmers. Cynthia Selfe (Chapter 12) is especially adamant about the benefits that accrue when professional educators do the program design and fully trained students actually write the program. For larger programs like those described in the second half of the book, this may in fact be the only practical method. But for those in our profession who wish to develop less ambitious projects, the computer itself is clearly not an obstacle.

How Are These Programs Produced?

The division of labor between program designer and program "coder" brings up the question of how programs like the ones described in this book are produced. This is of course a subject covered in each chapter, but some general observations are possible.

Because the size, scope, and purpose of these computer writing projects varies widely, there are many differences in program development. In some cases developers worked alone, in some cases as part of teams. In some cases the project was the beneficiary of foundation support (NEH,

FIPSE, Exxon and the Apple Education Foundation), but just as often the project was unsponsored. In many cases developers had the encouragement and help of department chairs or deans, but just as often colleagues were neutral or even hostile to the project.

While the number of people involved and the funding and the moral support differed, the developers worked in amazingly similar ways. Most spent a small amount of time researching similar projects (1–10 percent of total development time), a small amount of time looking for funding (usually 2–10 percent), and a fair amount of time designing and programming (20–40 percent), but in almost every case the largest block of time was taken up by testing and rewriting the initial programs (30–65 percent). This large effort in testing and rewriting probably came as a surprise to the developers. That so much effort was put into testing indicates the desire of the developers to produce quality materials. But the time also shows that such quality doesn't come easily or automatically.

The extensive rewriting and testing are signs that software is a new and highly volatile teaching method. Even the people currently developing projects of this type are only now seeing much of its potential, and as they do, they redesign their efforts. If asked about the status of their projects, nearly every developer would likely respond, "Which version?"

What's Next?

The projects described here and elsewhere will change and give us many new approaches to teaching writing by computer. But these efforts aren't happening in a vacuum. Three forces are at work to enhance the development of new computer-assisted writing programs. First, there is the computer industry. Because this industry is known for its rapid changes, we can expect its developments to give us more power at a lower cost. Second, computer science research is beginning to open up new possibilities for us. And third, a large number of people in our profession are learning about computers. I'd like to discuss each of these three forces in turn.

Roughly half of the programs described in this book run on microcomputers. That's not particularly noteworthy until you realize that microcomputers didn't exist prior to 1977. Only five years later, over one million microcomputers were sold in the United States. According to market analyst Greggory S. Blundell (1983), in 1987 six million microcomputers will be sold worldwide. Not bad for a product only ten years old.

Why have microcomputers sold so well? Part of the reason is price, but much of the success is due to the power of the new micros. A good example would be a comparison of two generations of IBM computers.

According to figures compiled by DeVoney and Summe (1982), the IBM 360–40, the standard business computer of the 1960s and 70s, could cost as much as $497,000, required special electrical circuitry and air conditioning, needed a cadre of computer operators, all in addition to a $383 per month maintenance fee. IBM's Personal Computer, released in 1982, costs between $2,000 and $3,000, plugs into any wall outlet, operates at room temperature, can be operated by a child, and needs no maintenance contract. The difference in performance? The IBM Personal Computer has as much internal memory as the IBM 360–40, yet processes instructions more than three times faster!

Microcomputers are small, inexpensive, but powerful. That matters to us as English teachers. In order to use computers in writing programs, we need to have enough machines so that students aren't rushed. They should be able to come into a computer lab and have an hour or two hours or as many hours as they need to plan, write, and revise. That will only be possible if there are many computers available, and we will only be able to acquire large numbers if the prices of these units are low. Fortunately they are, and all projections indicate still lower prices—often dramatically lower.

But it's not enough for these computers to be cheap. They also have to be powerful. The kinds of tasks we ask a computer to perform put a tremendous strain on it. Let's say one of our students is typing an essay and decides to pause and have the computer check his or her spelling. The computer must first be able to remember the text typed in so far; this alone is no easy task. It then must load a spelling checker program that will instruct the computer to scan each one of the student's words individually and check it against a collection of correctly spelled words. If the word in the text doesn't match a correctly spelled word, the computer must either display a message on the computer screen or store the problem word to be displayed with all problem words later.

This is quite a task for the computer, but the real problem is time. If the scanning of each word takes more than a fraction of a second, checking the spelling in a student essay could take many minutes, more time than most students are willing to wait. So in order for any of the computer programs described in this book to be useful, they must work on computers that are not only cheap enough so that we can afford to make them available to our students, but also powerful enough to meet our very demanding requirements. Luckily, all market forecasters agree that computers, especially the microcomputers that are so convenient for education, will continue to increase in power.

This increase in power will be especially important if we are to move into some of the more promising approaches available to us through artificial intelligence research. You will remember that all approaches in use so far are based on either word processing, Nold's questioner, or Page's feature analyzer. While these are all useful, they miss one point—they cannot understand what a student has written. If cleverly designed, programs like Nold's and Burns's can guess what a student has written and *pretend* to understand, but they can't really understand. (See Chapter 1 for Burns's comic description of just how bad a misunderstanding can get.) The research of Page and others tells us that feature analyzers can go a long way towards determining if an essay is any good, but the analyzers can't tell us what an essay is about.

Some of the programs written by Roger Schank at Yale can. He and his colleagues have been working for nearly 20 years to develop computer programs that can understand English. Breaking knowledge down into what he calls scripts, goals, and plans, Schank (1970) builds programs that have data about certain events arranged into those three forms. Once that data is available to the computer, it can use it to "understand" English sentences or paragraphs or even whole stories about pre-programmed subjects.

Examples Schank lists in his many books are very impressive. If someone were to type in a short story including a restaurant scene, for example, one of Schank's programs could understand the story to the extent that it could answer questions about it. It could make such inferences as "the man came in because he was hungry," "the woman who served him was a waitress," "he left in a hurry and left no tip so the food must have been bad." Schank uses the computer's ability to produce such inferences as evidence of its understanding of sometimes very elliptical stories.

Schank's concept of knowledge based on scripts, goals, and plans is not unchallenged, but for our purposes it is enough to know that there is a whole branch of computer science research working on the problem of making computers understand English. Schank's approach may be the one that does it; maybe it will be someone else's. But we can expect that even if there isn't a major breakthrough, there may in time be computers that are able to understand what is typed into them.

Such understanding will not come cheaply, however. Artificial intelligence software currently under development requires huge amounts of memory and the most advanced circuitry to process all the information at a reasonable speed. That means that even if programs fully capable of human understanding were available tomorrow, they wouldn't run on a machine we could afford to buy and certainly not on a machine we could afford to make readily available to students. But perhaps in five years technology will be available to allow us to start putting together programs that not only tell students they overused passives and misspelled *a lot,* but also committed a logical fallacy in appealing for shorter semesters.

The third force compelling the computer developments in English doesn't depend on cheaper or more powerful computers or on the discoveries made by our colleagues in computer science. This force, the involvement of many, many more people in our profession in the use of computers, is already strong. One would be hard pressed to find a single high school or college English department that doesn't have *somebody* exploring computers.

The explosion of interest should change the uses of computers more than any technological development or computer science breakthrough. For we are a diverse profession, ranging from huge departments like that at UCLA to minuscule departments like ours at UW, Marinette, from highly research-oriented graduate departments to middle school programs struggling to bring children up to basic literacy.

That diversity will be reflected in the uses to which computers are put. Different areas of the English curriculum will be singled out to be computerized. New approaches to using the computer will be tried. Some of these approaches will only be useful to the department where they are developed; others will lead to frustration and disappointment; but many will awaken other departments to new possibilities and lead us in directions we can't possibly predict. We've already noted how Page's work with a clumsy punchcard feature analyzer has developed into very helpful programs such as those of Cohen and Von Blum. Thus, we can expect the work being undertaken today to be reapplied and rearranged on high school and college campuses across the country. The result should be surprising, and pleasing, to all of us.

It is for this inquisitive and creative group within our profession that this book was developed. I hope it will serve as a first step for, and as a continuing reference to, those who are beginning their attempts to harness this new technology to their own purposes. If it does, this book will have served its purposes and repaid its authors in full for their contributions.

References

Atkinson, R. C. 1969. Computerized instruction and the learning process. In *Computer-assisted instruction,* ed. R. C. Atkinson. New York: Academic Press.

Blundell, G. S. 1983. Personal computers in the eighties. *BYTE* 8: 166–82.

DeVoney, C., and R. Summe. 1982. *IBM's personal computer.* Indianapolis: Que Corporation.

Hiller, J. H., D. R. Marcotte, and T. Martin. 1969. Opinionation, vagueness, and specificity-distinction: Essay traits measured by computer. *American Educational Research Journal* 6: 271–86.

Lawlor, J., ed. 1982. *Computers and composition instruction.* Los Alamitos, Calif.: SWRL Educational Research and Development.

Nold, E. 1975. Fear and trembling: The humanist approaches the computer. *College Composition and Communication* 26: 269–73.

Page, E. 1968. The use of the computer in analyzing student essays. *International Review of Education* 14: 221–24.

Schank, R. C., and R. Abelson. 1977. *Scripts, plans, goals and understanding.* Hillsdale, N.J.: Lawrence Erlbaum Associates.

Skinner, B. F. 1964. Why we need teaching machines. In *Educational technology: Readings in programmed instruction,* ed. R. P. DeCecco. New York: Holt.

Wresch, W. C. 1982. Computers in English class: Finally beyond grammar and spelling drills. *College English* 44: 483–90.

Wresch, W. C. 1983. Computers and composition instruction: An update. *College English* 45 (Dec.): 794–99.

I Prewriting Approaches

The three chapters of Part I describe how the computer can be used to facilitate prewriting activities. In Chapter 1 Hugh Burns describes his early efforts with programs that guide students through the topoi of Aristotle. The chapter includes detailed descriptions of his programming techniques. Chapter 2 points out how nonlogical heuristics can help some students think more creatively about their essay subjects. Chapter 3 is a description of how Helen Schwartz has used Apple computers to help her students think more clearly about literary subjects. Her project also involves using the computer to record student interactions about writing projects.

1 Recollections of First-Generation Computer-Assisted Prewriting

Major Hugh Burns
Human Resources Laboratory, Lowry Air Force Base

Now I'll tell you something about machines in American history. . . .
Machines were meant to open the territory, not close it down. . . .
What's all this got to do with computers? you ask. I'll tell you. They
reopen the territory, that's what they do. . . . O pioneer.

Roger Rosenblatt

If we are witnessing the fourth generation of computer sciences, then we must be approaching the fortieth generation of the rhetorical arts. Yet, as writers and writing teachers, we have just begun to combine this pioneering technology with our collective rhetorical and teaching experiences. Not many years ago, many rhetoricians were afraid to touch a computer keyboard. How many are using word processing or, better, text processing now? How many are exercising their argumentative skills debating the merits of word processing software—WordStar versus Perfect Writer versus Easy Writer? Likewise, how many writers have noticed what excellent proofreaders and jargon detectors on-line dictionaries are? Today, most composition teachers would not legislate against an electronic dictionary any more than they would legislate against the *OED*. A tool is a tool is a tool, they argue, and most of them agree such computing tools, wisely used, will open new territories.

So, 20 years ago, only a few enthusiastic pioneers believed that computer technology and English education would develop a congenial relationship. Word processors, supplementary computer-assisted lessons, and even analytical concordance programs have shown English educators the value of the new technology by effectively removing some of the drudgery of writing, teaching, and scholarship. More and more, we have assumed roles of technological pioneers, discovering better ways to integrate writing, teaching, scholarship, *and* computing.

15

For me, such reflections illustrate the dynamics in English education during the past two decades. But what does all of this have to do with rhetoric and education? Both rhetoric and education were also meant to open territories—territories of the mind and the imagination. More specifically, the new computer literacy has led to renewed examination of teaching methods used to develop writing skills, and, in my case, an investigation of prewriting strategies. I offer this background—what Kenneth Burke would call the "scene"—so that I can recollect a few memories of the first generation of computer-assisted instruction in prewriting. First, I define the act of computer-assisted rhetorical invention. What did I have in mind? Next, I share two annotated runs of one of the prewriting modules. How are these prewriting packages used? I then show two practical subroutines that helped me envision these open-ended programs. And I conclude with five recommendations for designing and developing the second generation of computer-assisted prewriting programs.

Invention: Tensions and Intentions

The five rhetorical canons—invention, arrangement, style, memory, and delivery—have greatly influenced my teaching approach and course design. In my research, however, I have attended more to invention or the processes of discovering what we know and, more important, what we do not know. Although the processes of arranging, styling, remembering, and delivering ideas are crucial undertakings in writing and speaking, my investigations focused on the invention process and, in particular, three heuristics: Aristotle's topics, Kenneth Burke's pentad, and Pike's, Becker's, and Young's tagmemic matrix. During the early stages of my venture at the University of Texas, the computer was nothing more than the means for keeping the empirical methodology pristine; in other words, the computer would administer the experimental questions and store the writer's responses, and, in that way, control the experiment for teacher variability. Computer-assisted rhetorical invention was conceived simply as a program written to ask questions, to spur a writer's memory, and to encourage the well-prepared student.

Changing tension between ideas into integral, purposeful meaning is the alchemy of the invention process. Thus, when I began investigating in more detail the implications of computer-assisted invention, three specific goals became uppermost in my mind. I wanted to create an artificial, on-line situation in which writers would exercise with specific methods of inquiry—a kind of mental fitness center, software moments replicating heuristic tensions that would result in information, perspective, and insight about any topic. I also hoped to assist writers in discovering how they begin writing, i.e., formulate a method of thinking or approaching a topic. And I sought to change the kind of prewriting help students request from composition teachers. For example, instead of asking, "What should I write about?" they would ask, "Is it okay if I first describe the diversity of public opinions about this matter and then show the legal contradictions?"

All three of these goals were ambitiously and fantastically qualitative in the sense that it would be difficult to quantify the extent to which students better understood their own writing strategies. While I still believe these goals are right-minded, perhaps even noble educational aims, the problem was to determine how I would achieve such goals using a computer program.

First-Generation Runs and Willing Suspensions of Disbelief

The following paragraphs include parts of two runs of the TOPOI program, the invention software based on Aristotle's topics. TOPOI operates at the U.S. Air Force Academy on a VAX 11/780 minicomputer. TOPOI and other invention software is not limited to supporting English composition courses; it supports any student or faculty member who can type "INVENT" on a computer terminal. Such availability is one way the Academy encourages prewriting across the curriculum. These programs, therefore, truly supplement our writing courses. We do not use more than one class period to demonstrate the program, allowing enough time for the students to become comfortable with the terminals and the access procedures. Some students, especially members of the debate team, are particularly comfortable and enjoy the electronic brainstorming a great deal. But some other students find that these programs are not useful ways to prewrite. In this category are those students who cannot type well enough, who are disappointed because the program cannot help them with their content, and who have not been instructed well enough about the program or the computer. TOPOI and other INVENT programs necessarily demand a user's willing suspension of disbelief; without that, the programs fail. Therefore, I include parts of two runs that illustrate the software's strengths as well as its first-generation weaknesses. I interrupt the dialogues at intervals to comment on them.

We join the first writer, Wally, after he has signed on the computer, received instructions about "Garbage in, garbage out," reviewed the directions, and elected not to read a brief description of Aristotle's discovery system.

```
    NOW I NEED TO FIND OUT WHAT YOU ARE
WRITING ABOUT, SO WOULD YOU PLEASE TYPE
IN YOUR SUBJECT. I AM LOOKING FOR ONE TO
THREE WORDS.

    PROTEST AGAINST MATERIALISM

    HEY, THAT'S NEAT, WALLY! WE'LL HAVE A
GOOD TIME THINKING ABOUT PROTEST AGAINST
MATERIALISM.
```

In this sequence, I want the user to type in a noun phrase that will fit the syntactic slots in the questions that follow. That explains the restriction of one to three words. Plural subjects and subjects with two propositions (e.g., spiritualism versus materialism) will not be as syntactically accurate later in the program. After the student enters his or her topic, the program then offers a bit of encouragement or humor. In this case, the program has a file of three remarks, and only one is randomly selected and printed on the CRT—"Hey, that's neat. . . ."

```
    A COMMENT ABOUT PURPOSE:

    DURING THIS EXPLORATION PROCESS, YOU
WILL BE ASKED TO CLARIFY THE PURPOSE OF
YOUR PAPER ON PROTEST AGAINST
MATERIALISM.

    SO NOW WOULD YOU BRIEFLY DESCRIBE WHAT
THE PURPOSE OF YOUR PAPER IS BY
COMPLETING THIS STATEMENT: THE PURPOSE
OF THIS PAPER IS TO. . . . (LIMIT: ONE
LINE)
```

```
     EXPLAIN HOW THE MYTHS ABOUT
MATERIALISM COME ABOUT AND HOW IT HAS
IMPROVED THE WORLD

     ANYMORE?
     (IF SO, TYPE WHATEVER IT IS. IF NOT,
TYPE 'NO.')

     NO


     FINE, WALLY, YOU AND I WILL TALK AGAIN
ABOUT YOUR PURPOSE.
```

Most writers have a purpose in academic writing. In this program, there are three opportunities for prewriters to state and refine their purposes. This is the first opportunity; the other two opportunities are offered after the fifth and eleventh questions. The limit of one line on the CRT restricts the input to no more than 132 characters. These single-line purpose statements could be read for key words, but I did not design the program with evaluating purposes in mind. At this point, the program simply collects the writer's first intentions. The concept of asking writers whether they have anything else gives them another line to clarify their purposes. Many students at this point will complete the first statement with these words: "Pass this darn class and get on to more important things."

```
     RELAX NOW, WALLY, AND ENJOY THIS
BRAINSTORMING SESSION.

     WHAT SPECIAL EXPERIENCES MADE YOU
SELECT PROTEST AGAINST MATERIALISM AS
YOUR TOPIC?

     THE STUDY OF MEDIEVAL MAN, THE WAY IN
WHICH HE WAS LEAD TO BELIEVE AT THE
TIME, THE INFLUENCE OF THE CHURCH.

     THAT'S THE IDEA, WALLY. GIVE ME SOME
MORE INFO NOW.
```

<u>TAKING</u> <u>IT</u> <u>FROM</u> <u>THE</u> <u>FALL</u> <u>OF</u> <u>ROME</u> <u>THRU</u>
<u>THE</u> <u>MIDDLE</u> <u>AGES,</u> <u>AND</u> <u>MODERN</u> <u>EUROPE.</u>
<u>GIVING</u> <u>EXAMPLES</u> <u>OF</u> <u>IDEALS.</u>

TERRIFIC, WALLY!

ANYTHING ELSE?
(YOU CAN ADD MORE INFO, ASK A
QUESTION, OR GIVE A COMMAND—WHATEVER YOU
WISH.)

<u>THE</u> <u>ACQUISITION</u> <u>OF</u> <u>MATERIAL</u> <u>WEALTH</u> <u>WAS</u>
<u>LOOKED</u> <u>UPON</u> <u>AS</u> <u>A</u> <u>SIN</u> <u>AND</u> <u>EVIL,</u>
<u>CORRUPTING</u> <u>THE</u> <u>SOUL</u> <u>AND</u> <u>MIND.</u>

OKAY.
(I REPEAT QUESTIONS IF YOU TYPE
'REPEAT!')

The first question is selected randomly from a list of the ten easiest questions in the program. I wanted to give the writer the sense that the exercise was easier than expected and that the initial purpose of the program was only to draw out what she or he already knew about the subject. Wally answered this question three times. I think the power of the heuristic approach is confirmed if the writer feels a need to elaborate in response to a written question, as if the question were higher in the cognitive domain. Each time Wally finished his response and pressed the return key, the program attempted to "understand" his remark by looping through a "semantic stab" subroutine which I will explain in more detail later. In the dialogue above, this routine does not recognize what Wally has typed; consequently, the program prompts the inquiry only with motivational responses. Finally, each question sequence ends with one of ten random, parenthetical hints about the prewriting process (e.g., "Don't worry about spelling yet") or, as is the case here, a hint about using a "Repeat!" command in the program. We skip ahead now.

WE'RE MOVING RIGHT ALONG. HERE IS
QUESTION 8.

WHAT COULD BE CONSIDERED A RESULT OF
PROTEST AGAINST MATERIALISM?

EXPLAIN!

THIS QUESTION IS ABOUT CAUSES AND
EFFECTS, BUT YOUR ANSWER SHOULD JUST
MENTION THE EFFECTS, THE RESULTS, THE
OUTCOMES OF PROTEST AGAINST MATERIALISM.

FOR EXAMPLE, IF I WERE WRITING A PAPER
ABOUT EXERCISE, I WOULD WRITE ABOUT A
STRONGER HEART, A NEWFOUND ALERTNESS,
AND ANOTHER WAY TO SPEND MONEY (JOGGING
SHOES, TENNIS RACKETS, BICYCLES,
WEIGHTS, ETC.)

YOUR TURN, WALLY.

THE STIFFILING OF PROGRESS. TECHNOLOGY
HAMPERED BECAUSE OF LACK OF MATERIAL.
WEALTH IN CAPITAL.

I LIKE YOUR REASONING. GOOD WALLY, ADD
TO YOUR RESPONSE NOW.

IF THERE IS NO CAPITAL, THERE IS NO
INVESTMENT, NO PRODUCTION, NO PROGRESS.

OUTSTANDING, WALLY!

ANYTHING ELSE?

NO

OKAY.
(SEE IF YOU CAN USE SOME MORE ACTION
VERBS IN YOUR RESPONSE.)

Every question in the program can be explained further if the writer commands with "Explain!" as Wally has done here. These explanations are also printed under two other conditions: if a writer types a "what" question or a string with "*do*n*t *underst*." (A string is a programming term meaning a series of characters, in this case, letters of the alphabet. The asterisks in the string allow for and ignore extraneous characters. For example, the program would "understand" this sentence: "I really do not understand what you mean by a result of protest.") For ten questions, the program will also show a sample answer to the question on common topics such as human rights, college academics, solar energy, or, as is the case here, exercise and physical fitness. These models offer answers users can imitate—the servile copying idea. Notice Wally misspelled two words, but the program does not worry about it. I did not include a dictionary in these programs for two reasons: memory limitations and my intention to help writers recapture ideas in the rough.

. Also, in this sequence Wally used the word *because* and was branched to a remark that complimented his reasoning skills. The key-word routine does not understand Wally's reasoning process, only that he used the word *because,* a simple clue that he has subordinated one idea to another. Small stuff, perhaps, but his next induction seems to follow nicely. In this sequence, he elaborates once and elects to continue. Another random but seemingly appropriate remark about using more action verbs closes this sequence. Jumping ahead in Wally's electronically assisted dialogue, we find the following:

```
HERE IS YOUR NEXT QUESTION-NUMBER 12

WHAT FACTS ARE YOU UNLIKELY TO KNOW
ABOUT PROTEST AGAINST MATERIALISM?

WHAT WAS THE INTENT OF THE CHURCH TO
KEEP MAN FROM ACQUIRING WEALTH.

GOOD, WALLY. ADD TO YOUR RESPONSE NOW.

AFTER ALL THE CHURCH DID IT, WHY
COULDN'T MAN?

WELL, WHY NOT? REMEMBER WE ARE
EXPLORING, BRAINSTORMING!

TRUE, THE CHURCH DID NEED WEALTH IN
ORDER TO ACQUIRE POWER IN ORDER TO RULE.

SUPER, WALLY!
```

Aristotle liked this question; it is a tough one to answer because *we don't know what we don't know*. But if writers have answers, what then? Wally answers this question, admitting some ignorance but also defining a direction for his research. In his elaboration, he asks a "why" question about the content of his topic. Of course, the software knows nothing about Wally's interest in materialism, but has simply been programmed to answer all "why" questions with a "why not?" In this particular run, the "why not" response continues his inquiry, for Wally answers his own question with "True. . . ." I'm surprised how often a semantic miscue or, in this case, a stalling tactic in the program twists the electronic dialogue but still makes some sense to the user. Wally accepts his role as content specialist, not expert, and understands that these programs require a *most willing* suspension of disbelief.

When Wally finished, he left the computer lab with his computer-assisted dialogue—14 pages worth. And, more than likely, he was still thinking about the correlation of power, money, and ideal faith.

The second run points out the limitations of these programs. Again, I pick up the remarks of the writer, Glenn, after he has seen the introduction. He did not review the directions or the explanation of the heuristic procedure. In other words, he rushed right in—a trait many human beings exhibit from time to time.

```
    NOW I NEED TO FIND OUT WHAT YOU ARE
WRITING ABOUT, SO WOULD YOU PLEASE TYPE
IN YOUR SUBJECT. I AM LOOKING FOR ONE TO
THREE WORDS.

    LIFE

    LIFE, HMMMM! WILL YOU BE AMAZED BY THE
RECENT SCHOLARSHIP. BE SURE TO ASK THE
LIBRARIAN IN THE REFERENCE AREA.

A COMMENT ABOUT PURPOSE:

DURING THIS EXPLORATION PROCESS, YOU
WILL BE ASKED TO CLARIFY THE PURPOSE OF
YOUR PAPER ON LIFE.

SO NOW WOULD YOU BRIEFLY DESCRIBE WHAT
THE PURPOSE OF YOUR PAPER IS BY
```

```
COMPLETING THIS STATEMENT: THE PURPOSE
OF THIS PAPER IS TO. . . .

   REFUTE ARISTOTLE'S THEORY OF LIFE

ANYMORE?
(IF SO, TYPE WHATEVER IT IS. IF NOT,
TYPE 'NO'.)

NO.

   FINE, GLENN, YOU AND I WILL TALK AGAIN
ABOUT YOUR PURPOSE.

   RELAX NOW, GLENN, AND ENJOY THIS
BRAINSTORMING SESSION.

   WHAT IS THE OPPOSITE OF LIFE?

DEATH

   AHH, SHORT AND SWEET. NOW TELL ME WHY?
IN OTHER WORDS, ELABORATE A LITTLE.
```

This "short and sweet" remark appears when an answer is less than ten characters in length.

```
   LIFE IS BEING, DEATH IS BEING NO
LONGER

   THAT'S THE IDEA, GLENN. GIVE ME SOME
MORE INFO NOW.

   DEATH IS A NEW LIFE AND NOT THE END

   GREAT, GLENN!

   ANYTHING ELSE?
(YOU CAN ADD MORE INFO, ASK A
```

```
QUESTION, OR GIVE A COMMAND-WHATEVER YOU
WISH.)

WHAT IS LIFE?
```

At this point, i.e., the third elaboration, the program does not read for key words, so it does not catch the "*what*?*" string. The program also cannot answer content-based questions, and more trouble begins.

```
    YES, THAT SEEMS OKAY. YOUR TURN,
GLENN.

    NO! YOU DIDN'T ANSWER MY QUESTION!

    OKAY
    (TRY EXPLAINING A LITTLE MORE. LESS
PHRASES, MORE SENTENCES.)

    QUESTION 2-ONE OF MY ALL-TIME
FAVORITES COMING UP.

WHAT SPECIAL EXPERIENCES MADE YOU SELECT
LIFE AS YOUR TOPIC?

    DON'T GET OFF THE SUBJECT PAL, YOU
TELL ME WHAT LIFE IS   ALL ABOUT!

    FINE, GLENN. WRITE SOME MORE.

    YOU DON'T KNOW WHAT THE [expletive
deleted] I'M WRITING ANYWAY.

    IF YOU HAVE A GOOD ANSWER HERE, YOU
WILL PROBABLY WRITE A DECENT PAPER. BY
'SPECIAL,' I MEAN 'UNIQUE,'
'INTERESTING,' OR 'IMPORTANT.' THESE
EXPERIENCES DO NOT NECESSARILY HAVE TO
BE YOURS; YOU COULD PRETEND TO BE A
REPORTER.
```

```
WHAT ARE YOU THINKING NOW, GLENN?

I DON'T WANT TO BE A . . . REPORTER. I
JUST NEED SOME HELP IN
```

He hits the return key.

```
OUTSTANDING, GLENN!

ANYTHING ELSE?

YOU DIDN'T EVEN LET ME FINISH. LOOK
CHUMP, I CAN PLAY ROUGH TOO.

OKAY.

WE'RE MOVING RIGHT ALONG. HERE IS
QUESTION 3.

WHAT HAS BEEN DECIDED ABOUT LIFE TO
DATE?

IT STINKS AND YOURS IS ABOUT TO
END . . . I'M GETTING OFF THIS MACHINE.
```

Glenn left with four worthless but fun-filled pages, never to return again. Not only was his time wasted, he did not learn the kinds of prewriting questions writers can ask themselves. He certainly did not leave with good feelings about computer-assisted invention. He did not understand how the program could help him, and he willingly suspended too much disbelief. He expected the program to be smarter than it was.

Generally, however, the writers who use these first-generation prewriting programs to assist their inquiry have found the experience fruitful. Questionnaires indicate that most composition students want more help in the early stages of writing, but composition teachers do not have enough time to play Socrates to every student's Phaedrus. Most users believe that these computer-assisted lessons help them begin their papers; they feel "pressure" to answer questions since the program stops and waits for their answers. This interactive approach is better than the list of 26 questions I once gave my composition students. These dialogues also help writers to articulate, refine, and preserve their ideas, even if the questions ignore content in favor of perspective.

Thus, the ultimate aim in teaching invention with systematic heuristic procedures is intellectual effectiveness. Do these modules stimulate this intellectual effectiveness as well as or better than current instruction in invention? For most composition courses, I believe they do; at least, they supplement the instruction with interactive, if not personal, practice. The processes of rhetorical invention are basically actions and reactions. In these programs, the computer acts to create the tensions, and the writer reacts to create the intentions.

Strings: Routines for Great Unexpectations

Now, as promised, a glimpse inside the programs. When I wrote the INVENT modules, I knew that I could use a technique for key word searching, but the problem would be determining the strings that users might type when responding to the program. In closed software, the programmer knows the correct answer and can have the program loop through a variety of "right" answers. But, in the open program I envisioned for rhetorical invention, I could not respond to the correctness, adequacy, or quality of the response. Consequently, I decided to search for explicit commands that help the user direct the program's operation, e.g., STOP!, CONTINUE!, EXPLAIN!, REPEAT!, etc. Next, I had the string analysis search for implicit ways that users might ask for clarification, e.g., "*I*DON*T*KNOW*", "*WHAT*?", "*HOW*?*", "*CAN*?*". Again, an asterisk is a symbol that allows for extraneous characters in any defined string. I also analyzed the string for double propositions (i.e., "* [space] OR [space] *"), subordination as explained before (i.e., "*BECAUSE*"), content questions (i.e., "*?*"). Part of the challenge was determining how to line up these so-called "semantic stabs" in the program. For example, I had to look for *what* questions before I looked for the question mark alone since I had programmed responses for all *what* questions but had only programmed some artificial, positively reinforcing statements for questions without the interrogatives *what, why, how,* or *can.* I began to think of these routines as the primitive soul of the program—primitive in the sense that the program would attempt to determine first why the user *did not answer the question.* If prewriting users answered the questions with declarative statements, then the program would whir through these analyses and *not branch.* When that happened, the programs asked the user for more information and offered some encouragement. That is one reason that the old motto for

computer-assisted instruction—"Garbage in, garbage out"—applies so
well to open programming.

For those who might wish to try some open-ended programming
themselves, I offer the two following subroutines. To begin, one might
imagine that the program has just asked a question and that it branches
to a routine to determine whether the user asked for a more detailed
explanation of the question. In such an instance the programmer would
need to stack and analyze all of the strings one by one by one. Part of
this routine is shown in BASIC:

```
500 J$=''*EXPLAIN!*''
510 GOSUB 800
520 IF K1=1 THEN 2000
530 J$=''*WHY*?*''
540 GOSUB 800
550 IF K1=1 THEN 2200
```

What's happening here? In line 500, the program prepares to search for
the string "*EXPLAIN!*," goes to another subroutine in the program
(line 800) where the string is analyzed character by character, and then
comes back with a value for a variable called "K1." At line 520, the
program checks to determine whether K1 equals one; if so, the program
branches to line 2000, where it gives the user the explanation. If K1
equals zero, then the program prepares to search for a *why* question. If
this same subroutine finds the "*WHY*?*" string, then the program
would branch to line 2200, where the program prints out, "Well, why
not? . . ." The 23 semantic stabs loop and loop in this way. Deciding
what to search for is one of the more difficult assignments in developing
open-ended computer software. The programmer must decide between
fast or smart but slower software.

Here is the BASIC subroutine or algorithm at line 800 that matches
the key-word strings:

```
800 LINPUT I$    'PREWRITER'S ANSWER
810 IF I$='' '' THEN 800  'NO ANSWER, NO
    PROGRESS
820 W=1  'ASSIGNING VARIABLES NOW
830 K1=1
840 I=2
850 L=LEN (J$)  'LOOK FOR ASSIGNED J$
    BEGINS
```

```
860 Y=INSTR (I,J$,''*'')
870 T1$=MID$ (J$,I,Y-I)
880 Y1=INSTR (W,I$,T1$)
890 IF Y1<>0 THEN 920
900 K1=0  'SORRY, THAT'S NOT THE ONE
910 RETURN  'GO BACK FOR ANOTHER J$, OR
     PUSH ON
920 I=Y+1  'LET'S SEE THE NEXT LETTER
930 W-Y1+1
940 IF Y<L THEN 860  'CHECKS LENGTH OF
     J$
950 RETURN
```

These sixteen lines represent only one of a number of ways to check strings. The novice programmer or the curious English teacher should not be intimidated by its appearance because this routine does nothing more than figure out the length of the word or phrase, look at each character one at a time, assign a number to keep track of its position, and return a one if it finds the string or a zero if it does not find it.

The cleverness of open-ended programming does not lie in building such key-word routines but in anticipating the strings themselves and arranging them in an appropriate order. When I built the prototype program at the University of Texas, I listened for hours to cassette tapes of students answering questions from the three heuristics I was exploring. These taped sessions were tutorials: a teacher asked questions and the students responded. I was struck by how often the students asked questions such as "Why do you ask that?" "What do you mean by that term?" "Is it okay if I tell you about this experience I had?" "Can I answer that with an example?" Programming a computer to respond to such questions became one of the major challenges, and these two subroutines were invaluable.

Of course, these routines had flaws from time to time. If a student asked "can" or "is it" questions, then the program answered "Yes, that's okay" or "Yes, I think so." In other words, these programs just can't say no. Walking into the writing lab one afternoon, I remember seeing a printout with big letters scrawled across it—"My Kind of Machine!" The subject on the printout was premarital sex. The writer asked the computer: "Can I have premarital sex?" The computer, after a few picoseconds, responded: "Yes, of course." Great unexpectations! The response only proves how artificially intelligent these first-generation programs, and sometimes their programmers, can be.

Precollections for Second-Generation Computer-Assisted Invention

In the first generation of electronic Socratic dialogues, the computer program presented questions, provided explanations, allowed writers to write on a computer terminal, and printed a transcript of the interview. Besides having a transcript, writers benefited by breaking through the initial writer's block and by entering the incubation or subconscious stage of the creative process. Thus, computer-assisted prewriting helped some writers break through psychological barriers by providing a setting for recovering what they already knew about a topic.

What's next? Second-generation computer-assisted invention will be developed with a greater understanding of the research in rhetoric and cognitive psychology as well as a willingness to experiment with the emerging, bolder assumptions about instructional computing's capabilities. Five recommendations come to mind.

A writer's natural recursive habits will need to be accounted for more in future prewriting programs. Since invention occurs throughout the writing process, bridging the gaps between invention and arrangement, arrangement and style, and back again, ought to be incorporated in the design of composition software. Although worrying too much too soon about organization or standard written English will normally hinder creativity, second-generation prewriting CAI will allow writers the opportunity to organize ideas or proofread to discover words not in the computer's dictionary, perhaps even pointing out minor grammatical matters. The development of word processors as idea processors should lead naturally to improved thinking and articulate expression.

Prewriting programs soon will be developed with more attention to content and the audience of software. Commercialism, if nothing else, will drive this change as speculation in software will first supplement textbook instruction. For example, an open-ended, computer-assisted review could be assigned after a student completed a specific reading assignment. This lesson would offer students the opportunity to focus on the assignment and take notes. With a few exceptions such as some poetry- or story-creating software, not enough attention is being paid to a sequence of composition software for kindergarten through college. Designing future invention programs will attend more to reading levels, to attention spans, to assignments, to color presentations, and to hardware constraints. Teachers need the capability to modify programs to meet, in the best possible way, the needs of their students. For example, in a discourse analysis class, I once wrote a program in which the students examined the openings of three novels we were studying—*One Flew Over the Cuckoo's Nest, The Sound and the Fury,* and *A Farewell to Arms.* The student was asked on-line to explicate these texts, an explication based on Kenneth Burke's dramatistic pentad. When students finished the program, they had descriptions of the scene, act, agent, agency, and purpose—a grammar of the motives for three particular openings. Teachers should have a way to select and input their own literary selections, thus designing computer-assisted literary data bases. Such inquiry programs, by being linked to specific data bases, have the potential to direct investigations, to provide bibliographies, and to support unique curricula, especially in the humanities.

In first-generation invention CAI, the questions were selected randomly, and when a writer answered the question, another random question appeared. The next generation of prewriting software ought to allow for elaboration within the heuristic point of view: less randomness, more logical relationships. For example, if the program asks a writer to elaborate about the good consequences of a topic, then the program should do more than say, "Please add to your answer." Rather the software—programmed to track the discussion of good consequences—should prompt accordingly. For example, the program might say, "Brainstorming sessions on positive consequences sort easily into categories. There are economic, political, practical, even psychological consequences for your topic. Which of these do you think is the most important consequence? Why?" If the writer used the word *economic,* then another "economic" elaborator could be asked: "Speaking of economics, I was wondering if you would care to list a few of the monetary tradeoffs. It would be good to do that before I completely change the point of view." In such cases, the elaboration technique, while still open-ended, is more directed. Designing elaboration routines for each question would require more time and much more anticipation, but open-ended CAI without such rich subroutines will fall flat. From the teaching point of view, more directed elaboration sequences would help students better remember and better apply the various heuristics.

While the first-generation prewriting programs relied on language and writing, second-generation prewriting software will rely on more color, graphics, and sound. Evocative programs will allow for media-enriched Socratic dialogues. Imagine prewriting suggestions such as "Next I'll hum in my own electronic way the opening eight bars of the 'Aria Liebesfreud,' then I'll let you type in what you were reminded of as you heard it. Press return when you are ready to listen." The elaboration sequences then could be directed to the definition of *aria* and how it relates to what the student wrote, or the program could address the matter of audience and mood: how moods are created, altered, and sustained in music, in writing, or in the particular topic being investigated. Such invention productions are not far away, for writing always has had color, structure, and sound.

Finally, when writers think about the process of thinking, they are often befuddled. It is like teaching someone to walk: while we can walk well enough ourselves, we cannot easily describe how we do it. Second-generation prewriting software should allow students to explore and better define their own cognitive styles, although they might not easily explain their own mental habits. How does a writing teacher help students better define and modify prewriting habits? By giving them patterns, formulas, images, techniques, and, yes, positive and negative reinforcement. I'm not suggesting that a computer program should print a composition biorhythm chart, but I am suggesting that the interactive dynamics of this electronic medium, well programmed, can enlarge a writer's awareness of his or her own processes and model an inquiry method.

With these five final "precollections"—better rhetorical connections, better accounting for content and audience, better instructional and elaboration routines, better color, graphic, and sound integration, and better intuitive models of inquiry—I'll conclude. How well this analytical, computing machine helps us reopen educational territories depends entirely on how well educators use it. Machines are not pioneers; people are.

System Requirements

TOPOI runs on the VAX 11/780. A few microcomputer versions have appeared and microcomputer development continues.

Program Availability

The INVENT series of three programs helps writers prewrite by asking them questions about their topics. TOPOI is the program used for persuasive writing; its questions are based on Aristotle's 28 enthymeme topics, e.g., questions about consequences, public and private opinions, reasons, etc. BURKE is the program used for informative or journalistic writing; its questions are based on Kenneth Burke's dramatistic pentad, e.g., scene, purpose, act, agent, and agency. TAGI is the program used for exploratory and informative writing; its questions are based on the tagmemic matrix of Young, Becker, and Pike, i.e., particle, wave, and field. All are written in BASIC.

TOPOI runs on the VAX 11/780 and is available from the English Department at the Air Force Academy, Colorado 80840. BURKE and TAGI are available from George Culp, Computation Center/HRC, University of Texas, Austin, Texas 78712. Write the author for details of microcomputer availability.

All three INVENT listings are available in *Stimulating Rhetorical Invention in English Composition through Computer-Assisted Instruction,* University Microfilms, Ann Arbor, Michigan 48106 (#7928268). Or contact the author at this address: Hugh Burns, Major, USAF, Human Resources Laboratory, Lowry Air Force Base, Denver, Colorado 80230.

2 Computer-Based Creative Problem Solving

Dawn Rodrigues
Raymond J. Rodrigues
New Mexico State University

Of all the steps in the writing process, perhaps none is more ignored than prewriting. Despite the urgings of authorities such as Donald Murray (1972) that prewriting ought to encompass the majority of class time spent in teaching writing, teachers seem not to have flocked to the practice. In fact, at both the secondary and college level, the number of teachers who spend much time on prewriting remains discouragingly low. Teachers sometimes have a sound reason for their resistance: classroom management. Teachers note that they have to teach literature as well as writing, prepare students for standardized tests that do not include writing, and, at the college level, work within the constraints of a one-term course.

Given this situation, the advent of the computer as a writing tool opens a new world. Teachers' common plea that there isn't enough time to teach writing, much less gimmicky invention techniques, will become less convincing when computer-assisted invention programs such as those of Nold (1975), Schwartz (1982), Wresch (1982), and Burns (1979) become readily available. These programs demonstrate that computer-assisted instruction can bring to the classroom an opportunity for students to work at writing processes without taking time away from the instructor. Moreover, thanks to the computer's infinite patience, students are free to experiment with ideas without worrying about imposing upon the instructor and without the instructor's having to check absolutely everything the student writes.

These pilot programs demonstrate the fascinating range of the computer and allow the classroom management problem to be seen in a different context, for with them the instructor has available a tool which is, in essence, a working partner. These programs include a variety of invention techniques, ranging from developing subtopics, considering audience, and developing major attributes to the tagmemics of Young,

34

Becker, and Pike; the pentad of Burke; and the enthymeme topoi of Aristotle. Missing from this list, however, is an invention technique which has been used for years by industry, science, and the military—creative problem solving.

It is understandable that early computer-assisted invention programs omitted creative problem-solving techniques. Some composition specialists don't classify them as heuristics, and reject them as frivolous remnants of the Sixties. Odell (1978) and Young (1976) have argued that freewriting and other intuitive prewriting strategies are not heuristics, since, by their definition, the term *heuristics* refers to "systematic inquiry procedures" and "processes of conscious inquiry" (Odell, 146–52). James Kinney (1979) disagrees, insisting that freewriting and metaphor making are just as important as other strategies, and equally intellectual. He feels that students need to understand all kinds of heuristics in order to explore a topic fully, tapping both sides of the brain. The rationalist heuristics such as the pentad and the tagmemic grid are linear, left-brain exercises; freewriting, metaphor making, and creative problem solving are right-brain procedures that allow the writer an opportunity for spontaneous insights before focusing on linear form. Considering results of research on learning styles (Gregorc 1979) indicating that different students learn in a variety of ways, we feel that intuitive invention strategies should be available for students who profit from them and enjoy them.

The purpose of creative problem-solving heuristics is not to provide a finished product, but to stimulate ideas, to force people to think of possible solutions that might never occur to them—given the human tendency to be trapped by a concept and not be able to break free. James L. Adams (1980, 129) argues:

> One of the most important activities you should engage in is trying to free your unconscious to engage in creative thinking. If you brainstorm (or synect) or merely consciously force yourself to be creative (by use of lists or whatever), a strange thing happens. First of all, you usually find that if anything you are more successful. . . . The more creative thinking is done, the more natural and rewarding it becomes and the more the ego relaxes.

Thus, creative problem solving enables intellectual playfulness, taking students away from the task at hand to the fun of discovering ideas and allowing time for the topic to incubate. Used with the computer, it is non-threatening because students can erase whatever they say before making it public.

In the early 1970s many teachers tried creative problem-solving techniques in classroom discussions, but often with no direct applications to writing. Students generated ideas, but then they were free to forget them or use them in whatever haphazard way they chose once they sat down to write. The microcomputer can provide the framework for prewriting exercises based on creative problem solving, can guide the student toward an organized set of ideas for writing, and can provide the student with a hard copy of the ideas generated.

The most commonly used creative problem-solving technique is brainstorming. It generates ideas rapidly but often lacks a focus. Or, if focused, the fact of its being generated by a group often means individual ideas are lost or subverted. What we wanted were creative problem-solving techniques that could be used with relative ease by individuals and that could be programmed for the microcomputer (Rodrigues 1983).

A Program in Visual Synectics

A number of techniques were available. The one we chose to begin with was visual synectics, a technique that forces students to compare the proposed topic to items that they might normally never consider. Those items are selected prior to the comparison: the student selects a picture or photograph at random, lists elements present in the picture, and then begins the process of making analogies between the topic and each element identified. The program works as follows. After a brief explanation of the process which is about to occur, the computer asks the student to type in her or his name and the writing topic; it then directs the student to select a picture from a packet by the keyboard. The computer can generate a graphic display, but the necessary programming is time consuming and in any event actual photographs or paintings seem to provide more variety. The instructor can cut them out of magazines in quantity and can vary them from time to time so that the student does not always have to work with the same ones.

When the student has indicated to the computer that the picture has been selected, the program continues, as in this example:

```
DESCRIBE WHAT YOU SEE IN THE PICTURE.
TYPE A LIST OF WHAT YOU SEE, STARTING
WITH NUMBER 1.

1. A BEACHBALL
2. A BATHING SUIT
3. SAND
4. AN OCEAN
5. SUN TAN LOTION
```

TRY TO FIND SOME OTHER THINGS IN THE
PICTURE.

6. A GIRL
7. THE SKY
8. A VOLLEYBALL NET

OKAY, ROBERTO, NOW REMEMBER THAT YOU
WANT TO WRITE ABOUT THE TOPIC: NUCLEAR
WASTE DISPOSAL. I WANT YOU TO THINK
ABOUT HOW YOUR TOPIC, NUCLEAR WASTE
DISPOSAL, COMPARES TO A BEACHBALL.
PLEASE TYPE IN YOUR IDEAS.

ON THE SURFACE, THE PLANS SEEM SOLID,
BUT THERE IS A LOT OF HOT AIR UNDERNEATH
THAT SURFACE

NOW THINK ABOUT HOW YOUR TOPIC, NUCLEAR
WASTE DISPOSAL, COMPARES TO A BATHING
SUIT.

WE MAY DISCOVER THAT IT OFFERS US VERY
LITTLE PROTECTION

HOW DOES YOUR TOPIC, NUCLEAR WASTE
DISPOSAL, SEEM SIMILAR TO SAND?

JUST AS THERE ARE SO MANY GRAINS OF SAND
ON A BEACH, THERE ARE SO MANY THINGS TO
CONSIDER IN PLANNING TO DISPOSE OF
NUCLEAR WASTE THAT SOME OF THEM MAY SLIP
THROUGH OUR FINGERS OR NEVER BE
CONSIDERED.

The program continues to ask the student to compare the topic with the
elements listed from the picture until the student reaches the end. Some
of the analogies may be very difficult for the student to make, but the
idea of visual synectics is to stretch the mind in the hope of gaining some

insights, perhaps even a unique one, that will enable the student later to produce a composition that grabs the reader's attention. If the student cannot think of a response, the student can type in something like I DON'T KNOW or simply hit the return key. Initially, some students may type in garbage, just to have fun and to prove the superiority of the human brain over the machine, but inevitably that proves little and provides the student with no help whatsoever. When students realize that the computer is a tool designed to help them, they tend to plunge right in. The best approach for the instructor, when the student enters garbage, is simply to say nothing, for the student will receive no credit for that step of the process.

When the student has finished typing explanations of the basic analogies, the computer lists each explanation one by one and asks the student to elaborate upon it:

NOW, ROBERTO, IN WRITING ABOUT YOUR TOPIC, NUCLEAR WASTE DISPOSAL, YOU SAID, ''ON THE SURFACE, THE PLANS SEEM SOLID, BUT THERE IS A LOT OF HOT AIR UNDERNEATH THAT SURFACE.'' PLEASE EXPLAIN WHAT YOU MEAN.

<u>WELL, THE GOVERNMENT IS TALKING ABOUT</u> <u>PUTTING THE WASTE IN SALT DOMES</u> <u>UNDERNEATH CARLSBAD, FOR INSTANCE</u>.<u>NO ONE</u> <u>KNOWS WHAT WILL HAPPEN TO THAT WASTE IN</u> <u>THE FUTURE. WE MAY BE SAFE, BUT WHAT</u> <u>ABOUT OUR CHILDREN AND THEIR CHILDREN?</u>

WOULD YOU LIKE TO SAY MORE ABOUT THAT? (YES OR NO)

<u>YES</u>

PLEASE GO ON.

<u>THE CITY COUNCIL SAYS THAT SCIENTISTS</u> <u>SAY THE WASTE WILL BE SAFE FOR A</u> <u>THOUSAND YEARS, BUT I THINK THE COUNCIL</u> <u>IS MAINLY INTERESTED IN SHORT TERM</u> <u>ECONOMIC GAIN FOR THE COMMUNITY.</u>

```
THAT'S INTERESTING. WOULD YOU LIKE TO
EXPLAIN THAT MORE? (YES OR NO)

NO

OKAY, IN YOUR NEXT STATEMENT, YOU
SAID. . . .
```

One of the issues in writing such programs involves the tone that the computer takes. The computer can speak in a straightforward, no-nonsense manner. For example, Nold (1975) programs the responses WHAT IS THE MAIN POINT YOU WILL MAKE ABOUT (RESPONSE NUMBER 1)? and WHO IS YOUR AUDIENCE? WHOM ARE YOU TRYING TO PERSUADE OR CONVINCE? For students who view the computer as simply a device that is there to expedite what they have to do as an assignment, such a tone may be best. However, for students who are hesitant to write to begin with, particularly when the computer-assisted invention is something new, a more comfortable, even lighthearted, approach may be more effective. For example, Burns's program (1979) speaks in an enthusiastic manner: GOOD, TERRIFIC! AH, SHORT AND SWEET. We have observed that most students are not used to working with computers—although that is becoming less true at an increasingly rapid rate—so the personal touches that computers can give seem both to entertain and to interest people who work with them, including jaded classroom teachers. Even the simple matter of addressing the writer by name is an important element of computer programs.

Another consideration with respect to tone has to do with our view of the writing teachers. To be most effective, writing teachers should appear to students as helpful, concerned partners in the writing process, experts who facilitate that process and resource persons to whom the student can turn to for advice and skills lessons. The teacher cannot be flippant, but the teacher can be informal and casual in speaking to the student. That, it seems, provides the appropriate model for the tone of a computer program, one that we are trying to emulate. It also provides one more needed area for research.

After having led the student through the process of invention by means of visual synectics, and having encouraged the student to elaborate upon what may sometimes be rather far-fetched analogies, our program summarizes all the analogies and their elaborations. The student can take the printout home to study it for arguments that seem most promising. Then, having decided which to employ, perhaps with the advice of the instructor, the student can proceed to develop the writing into a full composition, using supplementary, linear invention techniques as needed. The student may also choose to return to the program at any stage in the writing process, since invention is by no means restricted to the prewriting stage.

Although we now have several creative problem-solving programs, this first program developed rather slowly for us. We began with only the most rudimentary knowledge about how a computer program works, but we looked upon this project as an opportunity to learn to program more effectively in BASIC. We decided that we needed a model of how such a program might work and found one in ELIZA, Version 3.0 IBM Disk BASIC Version for the IBM PC. ELIZA is an open-ended counselling program that is based upon Rogerian nondirective counselling techniques. This particular version happens to be unprotected—that is, we were able to run a copy of the entire BASIC program and study how it worked. Here is a sample of how ELIZA looks:

```
HOW DO YOU DO.

PLEASE TELL ME YOUR PROBLEM.

I WANT TO LEARN TO USE COMPUTERS IN
TEACHING WRITING

DO COMPUTERS WORRY YOU?

NO

WHY NOT?

THEY CAN BE A TOOL TO FACILITATE
STUDENTS' LEARNING

IS THAT THE REAL REASON?

THEY CAN ALSO MAKE THE INSTRUCTOR'S JOB
MORE EFFICIENT

I AM NOT SURE I UNDERSTAND YOU FULLY.

IF THE INSTRUCTOR CAN SEND STUDENTS TO A
COMPUTER TO WORK, THEN THE INSTRUCTOR
```

```
HAS MORE TIME FOR OTHER TASKS AND FOR
STUDENTS.
```

ELIZA is not designed to present a predetermined concept or to lead the responder in any particular direction. But its ability to pick up cues from what the responder types in and its conversational style intrigued us. We wrote a simple prototype of our programs, using only limited programming techniques. As our skills developed, we expanded the program options and introduced random files to store and retrieve student responses. The skills needed to develop one program were readily transferable to others.

In short, we taught ourselves, with no official funding, working at our computer at home. Simultaneously, the university decided to purchase IBM PC's for its departments and to establish several computer laboratory centers for students. The English Department uses one of these centers for students in a few composition courses.

Since the English Department's microcomputers are housed in the writing laboratory, we have had the opportunity to field test our programs with both basic and regular freshman composition students. Tutors in the lab direct students to the appropriate programs. Logs kept by both tutors and students have allowed us to determine which programs students prefer, which ones they choose on their own, which ones they use at tutors' suggestions, and which aspects of the programs, including instructional management, need improvement. By having basic writing students meet frequently in the lab during one of their regularly scheduled hours of instruction, we have gathered data that have allowed us to determine the effectiveness of using our invention programs as an integral part of a writing course (Rodrigues and Rodrigues 1983).

Using Computer-Based Invention Programs

We have found that students tend to work well with conventional heuristic or invention strategies in class *when those strategies are employed as classroom exercises.* However, when the students are left on their own, they tend to forget the strategies and move directly toward a draft. For experienced writers, this procedure is not necessarily bad, particularly for those who discover what they want to say as they write. But not all writers work that way, especially inexperienced writers. Despite students' admitting that they liked working with various invention strategies in class—perhaps because they were entertaining or a break from previously learned routines—the students seldom used them in their own "real" writing. They either forgot them, or, if they did remember them as broad strategies, they forgot the separate steps. Here the computer helps as a guide to invention strategies. Once the student has learned the invention strategy in class, the student can work through that process under the direct guidance of the computer.

In the College of Education, the situation has been slightly different. Because the most common microcomputers in the schools have been Apples, Radio Shacks, and Commodores, the Department of Curriculum and Instruction has had to use such computers to train teachers. The College of Education also established its own computer laboratory with Apples and Texas Instrument computers. As a result, we have had to produce several versions of our program. We now have one written in IBM BASIC for English course use and one written in Applesoft BASIC for demonstration purposes in graduate and undergraduate education courses and for possible use in the public schools.

We have presented the programs to high school teachers during in-service sessions, and they seem intrigued. Their major questions concern ways to integrate computer programs into classroom activities. Many of the teachers admit to never having tried creative problem solving as an invention technique or, in fact, never having tried to do much in the prewriting phase of the writing process. For the first time they are interested in trying prewriting techniques because they have begun to realize how the microcomputer can facilitate the techniques. Thus, the program may move some teachers away from a compulsive drive toward the finished product and toward writing as a process.

Variations on the Prewriting Programs

Where do we go from here? Clearly, not all heuristic and prewriting techniques will work for all students. Just as Bridwell (1982) is finding that a student's writing style influences the ease or difficulty of working with a word processor, so one particular invention strategy may hinder some students while freeing others. It seems that the logical procedure for an instructor is to provide as many invention techniques as possible for students, as well as to make it relatively simple for the student to use those techniques.

We have found it necessary to include explanations and examples of creative problem solving in each program (the student has the option to skip those explanations and examples or review them). Our next steps will be, first, to develop a series of additional creative problem-solving programs; second, to develop supplementary programs based on the most common linear and rationalistic invention techniques; and third, to consolidate all of the programs into a single program that will allow a student to select his or her preferred strategy.

One creative problem-solving strategy is the use of a matrix to force students to relate the subtopics of their theses. By doing so, they are able to discuss those interrelationships in their writing and also make the syntactic and semantic links that are so often missing in student writing. We hope that this program will encourage a greater number of interlinear connections as well as more interparagraph relationships.

The matrix may be used as a two-dimensional field when first taught to students and later is easily expanded to a three-dimensional field. Thus, we begin visually with what might be described as a two-dimensional square plane and then move to a three-dimensional cube. For example, suppose that the student has chosen to write about the topic, "Should Taxi Cab Drivers in El Paso Be Required to Pass an English Proficiency Test?" Through a group brainstorming or brainwriting process (Rodrigues 1983), the student might generate, with other students, the following list of possible subtopics to write about:

Spanish is used in Texas and New Mexico.

English is, in fact, the national language of the United States.

Tourists can't understand the taxi drivers.

Many people are bilingual.

People who live or travel in this area ought to learn to speak Spanish.

Anyone who works in the United States ought to be able to speak English.

If someone is truly bilingual, that person ought to be able to speak both English and Spanish well.

If you can understand a street address and know the city, it doesn't matter what language you speak.

How do we handle tourists from Mexico if the taxi drivers can't speak Spanish?

If they have to pass a test in English, they ought to be required to pass a test in Spanish.

At the computer terminal, students type in their lists and see the items juxtaposed in a way that forces them to relate the subtopics. For example, using the two-dimensional matrix, the computer will ask:

```
HOW DOES THE IDEA THAT SPANISH IS USED
IN TEXAS AND NEW MEXICO HAVE ANYTHING TO
DO WITH THE IDEA THAT ENGLISH IS, IN
FACT, THE NATIONAL LANGUAGE OF THE U.S.?
```

After the student types in a response, the computer will, of course, ask for an elaboration and then ask the student whether the student wants to say more or to proceed to the next juxtaposition of ideas.

Using a three-dimensional matrix, the computer might ask:

```
PLEASE TYPE IN YOUR IDEAS ON HOW THE
STATEMENT THAT SPANISH IS USED IN TEXAS
AND NEW MEXICO RELATES TO THE IDEA THAT
MANY PEOPLE ARE BILINGUAL AND THE IDEA
THAT IF YOU CAN UNDERSTAND A STREET
ADDRESS AND KNOW THE CITY, IT DOESN'T
MATTER WHAT LANGUAGE YOU SPEAK.
```

The mixture of subtopics has been generated by the computer after the computer has assigned all subtopics to three groups and then selected one item, at random, from each group. At times, the student will not be able to think of an appropriate response and so might type in "I don't know." Then, when the computer prompts "That's very interesting, please go on," the student might still type "I told you I don't know!" but on the third prompt the computer would say "Would you like to say more?" That would allow the student to move on to the next set of juxtapositions. As with all creative problem-solving techniques, the purpose is to stretch the possibilities of ideas, to compel the student toward new and greater insights. Often the technique does not work, but when it does, the depth of student ideas increases.

What will the master program with all these creative problem-solving strategies along with the linear invention heuristics look like? It will begin with the student typing the desired topic into the computer. Then, the computer will ask the student which subprogram he or she wishes to work with first. One set of subprograms will simply enable ideas to be listed. The student can then select a subprogram that allows those ideas to be placed into a basic outline form. Next, the student could elect to revise the basic outline form into thesis and topic sentences. If the student cannot think of many ideas to begin with, the student can elect to enter one of the creative problem-solving subprograms. A menu of heuristic or problem-solving approaches might look like this:

```
A. Visual synectics
B. Focused objects
C. Simple analogy
D. Two-dimensional matrix
```

```
E. Three-dimensional matrix
F. Particle, wave, or field
G. Action, actor-agent, scene, means,
   purpose
H. Who, what, when, where, and why
I. Chronological flow chart
```

If, at any point, the student bogs down with a particular invention strategy, the student can type in a command that returns the program to the menu.

For the instructor, such a master invention program will have several advantages. First, the instructor can depend upon the computer to guide students through invention strategies they have learned in class, thereby freeing the instructor for other classroom efforts that may be more necessary if the class is to move on. Second, if the instructor does not want the students to work with a particular strategy, the computer could be prompted not to list that strategy in the menu. And third, new instructors or teachers who are hesitant to use certain strategies in their classes, for whatever reason, may allow the computer to do so.

We are enthusiastic about the potential of the computer as a major tool for invention. It will provide a new flexibility for both students and teachers in composition classes, individualizing writing instruction to accommodate students' diverse learning styles. It may also have an indirect benefit: if computer-based invention proves valuable to instructors in other content areas, it may foster more writing across the curriculum.

References

Adams, J. L. 1980. *Conceptual blockbusting.* 2d ed. New York: Norton.

Bridwell, L. 1982. The effects of the use of word processors on written texts and composing processes: Case studies. Paper presented at the National Council of Teachers of English Annual Convention, Washington, D.C.

Burns, H. L. 1979. Stimulating rhetorical invention in English composition through computer-assisted instruction. Austin: University of Texas. ERIC Document Reproduction Service No. ED 188 245.

Gregorc, A. F. 1979. Learning/teaching styles: Potent forces behind them. *Educational Leadership* 36(1): 234–36.

Kinney, J. 1979. Classifying heuristics. *College Composition and Communication.* 30(4): 351–56.

Murray, D. M. 1972. *The Leaflet,* Nov., 11–14.

Nold, E. 1975. Fear and trembling: The humanist approaches the computer. *College Composition and Communication* 26(3): 269–73.

Odell, L. 1978. Another look at tagmemic theory: A response to James Kinney. *College Composition and Communication* 29(3): 146–52.

Rodrigues, R. 1983. Tools for developing prewriting skills. *English Journal* 72(2): 58–60.

Rodrigues, R., and D. Rodrigues. 1983. Computer-assisted instruction invention strategies. Paper presented at the Annual Meeting of the Conference on College Composition and Communication, Detroit.

Schwartz, H. 1982. A computer program for invention and feedback. Paper presented at the Annual Meeting of the Conference on College Composition and Communication, San Francisco. ERIC Document Reproduction Service No. ED 193 693.

Wresch, W. 1982. Prewriting, writing, and editing by computer. Paper presented at the Annual Meeting of the Conference on College Composition and Communication, San Francisco. ERIC Document Reproduction Service No. ED 213 045.

Young, R., 1976. Invention: A topographical survey. In *Teaching composition: Ten bibliographical essays,* G. Tate. Ft. Worth: Texas Christian University Press.

System Requirements

The creative problem-solving program runs on an IBM PC with at least 64K RAM and one disk drive. A second disk drive makes it easier for students to save their work.

Program Availability

Contact the authors.

3 SEEN: A Tutorial and User Network for Hypothesis Testing

Helen J. Schwartz
Oakland University

"But what do I write?" Students who ask this question used to annoy me. I thought they were asking for The Answer, despite my emphasis on their developing a personal response to literature. Then I realized they were probably asking a different question: "How do I support a thesis about literature?" In other words, they were trying to figure out the conventions or gambits for proving hypotheses in the discipline (Dillon 1981; Perkins 1981; Smith 1982). Some students learn the conventions of the discipline by imitating the method of lectures or texts (of literary criticism or an A paper). Other students, however, find difficulty applying approaches *they observe* to approaches *they employ* when they write.

To bridge this gap between passive and active learning, I wrote a computer program, SEEN, to help students create, support, and refine a hypothesis. The program can be easily modified for different kinds of hypotheses, as I will discuss later, but I'll explain how the program works by using the version I field tested. This first version deals with a typical assignment in a literature class: analysis of a fictional character. The program has three parts:

1. A tutorial in which the student creates, supports, and tests an hypothesis.

2. An electronic network (programmed in the software) through which the student can discourse with peers to refine ideas and learn about audience needs.

3. A textfile which accumulates a printable record of the student's activities and ideas, along with peer comments from the network on his or her ideas.

The program is a supplement to traditional methods of instruction. It not only tutors students in developing ideas about a particular literary work, but it helps them to internalize almost effortlessly the procedures appropriate for arguing evidence in a discipline. Furthermore, students' work can become the basis for individually chosen paper topics without taking hours of the teacher's conference time. Finally, SEEN can aid researchers in tracing an individual's cognitive development in a manner more convenient, less intrusive, and less costly than otherwise possible.

Theory and Sample

The name SEEN, an acronym for Seeing-Eye Elephant Network, refers to the program's three parts, each providing in the learning environment an element widely advocated in composition theory. The first part consists of a "seeing-eye" tutorial. Here, the student builds on his or her personal response to literature, as advocated by Rosenblatt (1938) and Britton et al. (1975), by creating an hypothesis about a fictional character. (The program prompts the student to choose a character X and create an hypothesis Y.) Then, in open-ended questions incorporating this hypothesis ($X = Y$), the program prompts the user to supply different kinds of evidence, in effect introducing the conventions of evidence in the discipline. Thus, the tutorial provides a method of analysis or "heuristic" (Winterowd 1975; Young 1978).

The ideas developed and recorded in the tutorial are posted under the student's chosen pen name as a "notice" on the second part of the program, a computer-managed network. Here student writers enter a "universe of discourse," giving them a real sense of audience for developing and refining their ideas (Moffett 1968; Emig 1971; Kroll 1978). On the network they can read each others' "notices" and make and read comments on the "notices." The learning environment is nonthreatening because only pen names are used. But students are also responsible, first, because everything is "signed" with pen names and, second, because each student has anteed up a notice and thus has a stake in the game. (At later sessions, the program starts the student on the network, listing all notices and comments, and then gives the student the choice of going back to the tutorial.) Finally, pressure on students is low: they can work at their own convenience and at their own pace, without the pressure of a large class or a "fast track."

The "elephant" part of the program compiles a cumulative record for each user in a printable textfile. An individual's file includes a record of her or his activities, all notices generated in the tutorial, and any comments accruing to those notices on the network. Students can thus trace the development of their ideas, a reflexive or metacognitive approach useful in generalizing learning (Ford 1981).

Let's look at how a student (pen name Zapion) actually used the program in a large, introductory class on world literature. Her work on

Don Quixote spanned three weeks, including class discussion, two SEEN sessions, and an essay examination. At her first session on *Don Quixote,* Zapion went first to the network since she had already written a notice. The program gave a list of notices and comments:

```
     ***LIST OF NOTICES AND COMMENTS***
NOTICE 1 = SANCHO PANZA IN DQ IS NAIVE
SAYS KAMI

          COMMENT 1.1 BY ZACH
NOTICE 7 = HAMLET IN HAMLET IS HUMOROUS
SAYS ZAPION
NOTICE 9 = DON Q IN PART I = CRAZY
(MENTALLY) SAYS TELFON
```

The program has room for 12 students per group. No students were using slots 3 and 4. Notice 10 was mangled by a program bug, and I have omitted five notices on *Hamlet* and one on *Sir Gawain* to save space.

A program menu then gave Zapion the choice of using the network, going to the tutorial, or ending the session. Zapion looked at all of the notices and comments in order. On *Don Quixote,* she first saw Kami's notice arguing that Sancho Panza is naive. Zapion added more specific evidence, along with the following modification of Kami's hypothesis: "Sancho is escaping all the horrors of living in poverty, if only for a while. He receives rewards better than any material gifts Don Q could give him. He shares some profound thoughts with others and gains confidence in himself."

Later in the same session, Zapion began her definition of eccentricity when she saw Telfon's rather thin, derivative notice arguing that "Don Quixote (Part I) is crazy (mentally)":

```
BECAUSE OF WHAT HE DOES: HE DECIDES ON
THE SPUR OF THE MOMENT THAT HE IS GOING
TO RIGHT THE WORLD'S WRONGS. HE HITS THE
TWO MULE DRIVERS WITH HIS LANCE. HE
BELIEVES THAT ANYONE COULD HAVE DUBBED
HIM AS A KNIGHT.
```

```
BECAUSE OF WHAT HE SAYS: HE REFERS TO
THE TWO GIRLS AT THE SO-CALLED CASTLE AS
DAMSELS.

BECAUSE OF HOW OTHERS REACT: THE
INNKEEPER WENT ALONG WITH HIM BECAUSE HE
THOUGHT HE WAS CRAZY. THE TWO GIRLS
LAUGHED AT HIM WHEN HE CALLED THEM
DAMSELS.
```

Zapion then looked at the comments on the notice—Telfon's additional information on his own work and Zach's rebuttal to Telfon:

```
TELFON: HE MISTAKES SOME WINDMILLS FOR
GIANTS DESPITE SANCHO PANZA'S EFFORTS.
HE ALSO MISTAKES TWO HERDS OF SHEEP AS
ARMIES.

ZACH: BUT IS HE REALLY CRAZY WHEN HE
SAYS I KNOW WHO I AM AND WHO I MAY BE,
IF I CHOOSE-IT COULD BE THAT HE KNOWS
EXACTLY WHAT HE IS DOING. HE ALSO GIVES
GOOD STABLE ADVICE TO DON DIEGO ABOUT
HIS SON AND A CRAZY MAN COULD NOT HAVE
DONE THAT.
```

Zapion then added her own modification to the hypothesis: "There's a line in a song that says, 'I've always been crazy, but it's kept me from going insane.' We don't know very much about Don Quixote's life before he read the books. Maybe acting crazy is the way he chooses to keep from going insane!" In both her comments, Zapion has begun the motifs on economic influence and the definition of craziness which run throughout her work on *Don Quixote*.

At this same session, Zapion also chose to go to the tutorial. There the program asked her to choose a character (she chose Don Quixote), name the work, and then describe the character in 20 spaces or less ("eccentric"). After creating this tentative hypothesis (Don Quixote is eccentric), the seeing-eye tutorial prompted Zapion to support her view with different kinds of evidence.

WHAT DOES DON QUIXOTE DO THAT SHOWS DON
QUIXOTE IS ECCENTRIC?

He has nothing else to do with his time
but read books, in the beginning. He
does so many strange things without
seeming to care for his own well being.
He can take off on his adventures
without worrying about bringing money.
He wills all his money to his niece.
Only if she doesn't marry a man who
reads books about chivalry.

Zapion struck a carriage return to end her response to the question. A
carriage return produces these options:

TYPE L (TO LIST), A (TO APPEND), D (TO
DELETE), C (TO CHANGE), E (TO EXIT), OR
PRESS RETURN TO CONTINUE.

Zapion chose to continue.

WHAT DOES DON QUIXOTE SAY THAT SHOWS DON
QUIXOTE IS ECCENTRIC?

Almost every time he opens his mouth
it's to recite some lengthy speech. He
speaks to people in a manner that makes
them something they're not.

HOW DO OTHER CHARACTERS REACT TO DON
QUIXOTE WHICH SHOWS DON QUIXOTE IS
ECCENTRIC?

The owner of the hotel and a few others
go along with him to amuse themselves.
Sancho Panza travels all over with him
thinking that he may receive a reward.
Don Diego knows that there's an

```
intelligent mind underneath the
foolishness.

HOW DO OTHER CHARACTERS (IN A SIMILAR
SITUATION) ACT AND HOW DOES THIS
COMPARISON SHOW THAT DON QUIXOTE IS
ECCENTRIC?

Sancho Panza tries to inform Don Q of
his misinterpretations. He sees the
reality that Don Q is refusing to see.
Howard Hughes did a lot of strange
things like Don Q!

IN DON QUIXOTE, IS THERE A 3RD PERSON
NARRATOR (Y/N)? YES

WHAT DOES THE 3RD PERSON NARRATOR SAY
WHICH SHOWS DON QUIXOTE IS ECCENTRIC?

He seems to make fun of Don Q often.
```

Here the program lists the notice so far and gives Zapion a chance to
change it. SEEN then prompts the user to test and refine evidence and
ideas as follows:

```
OK, NOW TRY TO THINK OF ANY EXCEPTIONS
OR CONTRADICTORY EXAMPLES.
WHAT EVIDENCE SHOWS THAT DON QUIXOTE IS
NOT ECCENTRIC?

Sometimes he seems to know exactly what
he is doing.

AT THIS POINT DO YOU WANT TO
1 = EXPLAIN THE APPARENT CONTRADICTION
2 = ADD THE EXCEPTION WITHOUT COMMENT
DO YOU WANT 1 OR 2? 1
```

```
OK, ZAPION, COMPLETE THE FOLLOWING
SENTENCE:
SOMETIMES HE SEEMS TO KNOW EXACTLY WHAT
HE IS DOING, BUT . . . I think that's
how eccentric people act.
```

At this point Zapion can write a new notice, go to the network, or (what she actually did) end the session.

Although the program may appear to know what the user is saying, in fact it does not. It picks up and uses designated pieces of information (name of the character, literary work, hypothesis) in questions based on the conventions of evidence in the discipline in the same way that the ubiquitous magazine sweepstakes letter picks up my name from a mailing list and then inserts halfway through the letter the exciting news that "you, Ms. Schwartz, may already be a winner!" The program does not and cannot check answers; that is the job of users.

The really original part of Zapion's approach concerns the role economic status plays in an assessment of Don Quixote—as seen in the way he initially has the leisure to spend his time, his selflessness, the specifics about money in the "does" section, the reference to Howard Hughes, and the choice of "eccentric" as an hypothesis. The chronology of Zapion's evidence is rather jumbled and the evidence about what Don Quixote says is vague or merely suggestive rather than specific or argued. Still Zapion has found a basis for believing, especially in the "others" section, that Don Quixote's eccentricity is not harmful to others and that it doesn't prevent them from interacting with him. Nevertheless, Zapion insists on Don Quixote's unreality in the "compare" section comments about Sancho Panza. The notice isn't smooth or internally coherent, but a balanced view of Don Quixote is emerging.

At her next session, Zapion worked mainly on *Paradise Lost,* but she also saw two notices on the character of Don Quixote. In response to one, Zach's excellent argument that the Don was wise and true, Zapion agreed in a touchingly responsive comment: "Sometimes Don Q reminds me of an innocent child . . . He trusts and finds goodness in everyone."

Before the exam, Zapion got a printout of her textfile. That included her notice on Don Quixote but no comments, since the network had been stripped ("reinitialized," in computer jargon) shortly after she wrote. She also got a summary of her activities at each session:

```
11/4 User #7 Activities: 1, 1.1, A1.2,
2, 5, 5.1, 5.2, 5.3, 6, 6.1, 6.2, 6.3,
```

```
8, 8.1, 9, 9.1, 9.2, A9.3, 11, 11.1, 12,
12.1, 12.2, NTC
```

This showed me Zapion had looked at every available notice (given in whole numbers) except her own, had looked at every comment (given as decimal numbers), and had added the second comment on notice 1 (A1.2) and the third on notice 9 (A9.3) before writing her notice (NTC) on Don Quixote. This listing assured that she got credit for her session, even if program bugs destroyed a notice or comment. It also allowed me to trace her thinking.

On the essay exam several days later, Zapion included the thesis about eccentricity in her essay on the madness of Hamlet and Don Quixote.

> Both men are considered to be mad because they speak and act contrary to what everyone else believes to be proper. Don Quixote . . . sees real objects and perceives them to be different according to how he feels they should fit into each scenario. He involves people, places and things in these daydreams. . . .

The essay shows an excellent, thoughtful, "owned" hypothesis. Zapion was engaged with the topic, and though not necessarily original, her ideas had been thoroughly digested from discussion and redeveloped as her own. However, since the essay lacks the consistently specific evidence that I was requiring for an A grade, Zapion earned a B.

After the exam, Zapion continued to look at and respond to notices on Cervantes's eccentric hero even though she would not be tested further on that work. Zapion often looked at all the notices, so it's hard to argue from her behavior that SEEN encourages passionate involvement with the subject. A more telling example, however, is Telfon. He was less involved and responsible than Zapion, yet he continued to look selectively at notices about characters he'd studied even after the final test on a character.

Classroom Management

SEEN was first used with volunteers in connection with an introductory college course in world literature that I taught at Oakland University. Of the 120 students registered for the course, 40 volunteered to use the program. I trained them in 30-minute demonstrations to use the computer. Thirty-eight of the volunteers fulfilled their "contract" to use the program for a half hour per week for a minimum of nine weeks.

Since a user had to write a notice each time the system was stripped of data and restarted, this meant the students had to write at least five notices during the semester. Otherwise, students were free to use SEEN as they pleased—to write or modify their own notices with the tutorial, see others' notices, write or see comments on the network, or do a combination of these functions.

Careful scheduling assured that each student had at least a half hour per week reserved at a convenient time. Additional time was available on a first-come, first-served basis to allow for make-up or additional sessions. Students worked in groups of up to 12 students, with one group disk for shared data and another disk for every one to six users to store individual textfiles. Disks were stored in a central location to facilitate sharing disks and printing out student files. In this manner, 38 students used one microcomputer—an Apple II Plus with 48K, DOS 3.3, and one disk drive—to fulfill the computer part of their contract.

My ability to trace the use of the program led me to make a number of revisions. I will explain the revisions later in this chapter. For now, let me raise a few of the questions and issues the instructor faces when using the program in the total learning environment.

Can SEEN Be Used with the Whole Class?

With a large class, I foresee problems in scheduling adequate access to computers and keeping track of many group disks. (I have students take responsibility for the disk with their personal textfile.) In small classes, scheduling is easier.

Should Use of SEEN Be Required?

I feel strongly that CAI should be a playful, optional activity. Computer anxiety can be real, especially—I've noticed but hate to admit—with mature students. Thus, even though the program is easy to operate and has overcome computer anxiety in novice users, I cannot bring myself to require use. I also have logistical considerations to take into account: I cannot require computer work in addition to classroom work at a university where 75 percent of the students are commuters.

On purely pedagogical grounds, I don't think SEEN should ever be more than an option. Some students, especially at the extremes of ability, do better with individual or group conferences, and journals are probably more effective for very reticent students. And the timing should vary, even with volunteers. Bright students should be weaned from SEEN and onto a word processor or into regular essay writing after about four weeks' work with the program.

Should There Be Credit for Work with SEEN?

Again, CAI should provide a playground for ideas, a place without serious consequences. I feel that the whole purpose and value of the CAI program would be undermined if students were graded on the quality of their work with the program. Although students knew I could and did look at their work, they also knew that the CAI contract was only quantitative. I believe the absence of qualitative judgments of their CAI work played an important role in their using SEEN for active learning—that is, as a vehicle for exploration, discovery, and intellectually serious playfulness. Ideally, students should use SEEN as but one of a number of options in part of a *process;* their grade, however, applies to the *product*. In a small class, for example, use of SEEN could be a prewriting option.

I have used SEEN as an option without extra credit; instead, users were allowed to write only the essay part of in-class exams. This did not work to the advantage of some students who did better on short answer and objective sections; for them I chose the higher of two exam scores: double the essay question score or double the total score.

Does SEEN Mean More Work for the Instructor?

There is a certain amount of time (and, for novices, frustration) involved in setting up the program. Some of this can be done by others if you have assistance from a computer center or computer freaks in your class. If not, the time averages out to about an hour extra per week. Other jobs, which I did during the field test, I would now farm out to others, for instance, training students to use the computer and print their textfiles.

I spent virtually no time participating in group work. I monitored group work only for program bugs and logistical problems. (I became a user in each group, making my presence clear in my notice: TEACHER IN ENGLISH 100 IS READY TO HELP SAYS SNOOPY.) As I was printing out textfiles, I would read them and comment. As I analyzed the results later, I realized that many students were excellent commentators. I, on the other hand, always sounded like the teacher: "How does Satan compare to Eve in this regard?" I also realized I was missing a real opportunity to individualize instruction. I encouraged students to develop *their* personal responses in SEEN and then tested them by springing *my* unannounced topics on them. But during printout time, I could have read and proposed to each student an exam topic demonstrably of interest to him or her.

Description of Results

To date, study of the program's effects is more descriptive than evaluative. Data include responses to student questionnaires, textfiles of student work, and students' essays and grades on exams. This section describes observations about student use of SEEN and the modifications I subsequently made in the program for more effective use. (Readers should keep in mind that CAI users were volunteers, a condition which may have affected their behavior.)

Students used SEEN in responsible but various ways, adapting the program to their own needs and personalities. They sometimes came to the tutorial with an argument already thought through; at other times they were more exploratory and tentative. The notices themselves showed three basic patterns: listlike notices simply reviewing facts; coherently argued responses; "Eureka" notices in which a student started listing and then appeared to discover an argument that gave coherence to what followed. Students tended to write notices that conformed to one basic pattern, although most users departed from their pattern at least occasionally.

In the tutorial, the "management" decision to supply discipline-specific prompting questions seemed effective. The heuristic not only freed the student to direct attention to his or her perceptions of the literary work, but it also resulted in the internalizing of those questions—and the discipline's conventions of evidence—in a natural and an accelerated way. Responses on student questionnaires after the final exam suggest that students internalized the tutorial's questions so that they *read differently* and perceived more as they went along (according to 33 of the 37 students responding).

A few comments illustrate repeated themes on the questionnaires: "It helps me analyze my feelings on characters even when I'm not actually typing them into the computer. I find myself looking for facts on characters as I'm reading the story through even the first time. I understand content of story better as I find these facts." And, "Seeing others' opinions and formulating my own has been extremely helpful and fun. It makes the essay exams much easier, almost enjoyable! I wish more classes could have a format like this."

As the last comment suggests, students also adapted the network to their individual needs. According to questionnaire responses, a student who had not read Work A would sometimes read other students'

notices about Work A as a way to direct or preview his or her subsequent reading. Some students concentrated on the tutorial, largely ignor-
ing the network and seeing only comments on their notices provided
with the printouts. However, most students combined tutorial and network activities.

Two of my fears regarding student use of the network were not
realized. First, students did not plagiarize. Instead, they used others'
evidence as the subject of their appended comments or as arguments to
be integrated as part of their subsequent notices. In effect, they were
using the work of their peers as secondary sources in literary criticism.

Second, they did not pick up inaccuracies from other students' work in
a forum that was largely unmonitored by an instructor. Comments on
questionnaires suggested that students were judging the rightness of their
ideas in comparison to others' views. In fact, careful analysis of the actual
notices shows that there were very few clear errors to *be* picked up. There
were vague or misleading statements, but most were accurate or at least
arguable. And many students felt free in the safe network environment to
rebut (politely but often intensely) or to modify or qualify what others
had said. This tended to enrich the context of arguments, promote personal response and involvement, and help students refine their perceptions.

One effect, almost too subjective to be treated as data, was especially
rewarding for me. I don't think I'm an aloof teacher under normal circumstances, but using SEEN seemed to increase even more my liking for
my students as people. Perhaps I just appreciated their cooperation
despite bugs and glitches of various sorts. But I got to listen to them
more regularly and more informally than usual. I found that Telfon
probably didn't do a very good job with the reading assignments, when
he did them, although his test scores would not have kept this secret.
But I was excited to see him start wrestling with the question of fate
and will: Could Satan have done anything differently in *Paradise Lost*?
Furthermore, my computer acquaintance with 40 students in a class of
120 made the whole class feel I knew them better. Overall, I felt I became
a better and more humane teacher as a result of knowing more intimately
how my students think.

The effect of SEEN on student essay writing is difficult to assess.
Overall, the average scores of the CAI users increased slightly on each of
the three exams after the pretest (taken before they started using SEEN),
but the achievement of individuals (as opposed to the group average)
varied widely. In short, improving the students' perceptions in support of
hypotheses did not necessarily improve their selection and organization
of ideas on the essay exams.

Modifying SEEN

This final observation suggested three modifications of the program and its use. Perhaps it is simply wrong to think that improving students' perception of evidence will improve their arguing of evidence. The questions in the tutorial do not set up an essay format. That is, no one argues that Don Quixote is eccentric by discussing first what he does, then what he says, and so on. One way around this problem involves programming the questions in a form that fits the question. This was the case with the adaptation programmed for an art history class, discussed later in this chapter.

However, students should be encouraged to bridge the gap between perceiving and arguing evidence by generalizing the insights discovered in the tutorial and finding the shape of their argument. Therefore, two questions have been added to the tutorial. The first asks the student whether the character changes in the course of the work; if so, the user is invited to explain how and why. This makes explicit the chronological element that may be important in a characterization and which was only hinted at in the original version when exceptions were considered. The second new question ends the tutorial by asking the student to summarize her or his ideas and their significance. This encourages the student to integrate evidence into an argument.

If the point of SEEN is to encourage personal response and active learning, then it may be counterproductive to test students with previously unannounced questions based on what the *teacher* feels are issues. With SEEN, teachers should be able to individualize essay questions, without hours of conference time or fear of plagiarism. While monitoring student printouts, a teacher can simply circle a hypothesis or question in a notice or scribble a topic in the margin of the printout.

A third change may also improve SEEN's effectiveness for improving student writing. I've reprogrammed SEEN in Applesoft BASIC, storing the students' work as files that can be loaded onto a word processing program. Furthermore, student entries are no longer limited to two lines. Therefore, students should be able to write something more like a rough draft, especially in answering the last two summary questions.

SEEN is now being modified to allow users a choice of tutorials. A second version of SEEN, programmed as an aid in an art history class, illustrates how this can be done. Charlotte Stokes of the Oakland University Art History Department designed the questions while maintaining the basic structure of SEEN. The new version asks the user to pick a work of art and then hypothesize about the period or style of art it illustrates. Then the program prompts the student to supply evidence of why Work X exemplifies Period Y because of the artist's (1) choice of subject, (2) use of color, (3) arrangement of forms, (4) exploitation of the medium, and (5) treatment of the human body (if any appear in the work). Other tutorials on plotting and symbolism as well as a unit on history are currently under development.

Production of SEEN

I started work on the program in fall 1980 during a sabbatical semester funded by Oakland University and spent working in conjunction with Project Solo/NET/work, a National Science Foundation Educational Project, directed by Thomas A. Dwyer at the University of Pittsburgh. I worked independently but was much influenced and inspired by Dwyer's work, especially in collaboration with his associate, Margot Critchfield. When I arrived in Pittsburgh, I had studied FORTRAN, but I learned BASIC from Dwyer and Critchfield's text *You Just Bought a Personal What?* as I read up on composition theory and researched CAI applications in English studies. I was especially intrigued with applications that prompted users with open-ended questions (Nold 1975; Burns and Culp 1980). My continued research on applications resulted in a *College English* article, "Monsters and Mentors" (1982). This combination of theory, example, and programming, set in a supportive environment, led to my conceptualizing the whole program and writing the tutorial. Originally called MARSY/EBB, an acronym for Mentor and Recording Secretary/Electronic Bulletin Board, SEEN benefited from the assistance of Bob Hoffman and Blaise Liffick of the Solo/NET/work staff.

I resumed teaching at Oakland in the winter of 1981 and had no time to finish the program until summer. Then colleagues in Engineering let me use their equipment and pick their brains. A graduate assistant, Raman Lakshmanan, helped me with the intricacies of Microsoft BASIC, and Ron Mourant, a professor in Engineering, became a resource person for advice on grant writing and lab operation, two areas of expertise foreign to most English teachers but useful for CAI work. I also established friendly and cooperative relations with technical staff, especially Len Brown, who have repeatedly and reliably helped me solve computer problems ever since.

Once SEEN was programmed, Oakland University supported my efforts to integrate computers in instruction, with then Acting Provost Keith Kleckner giving me one Apple and Acting Dean Jack Moeller arranging release time for fall 1981, when I first used SEEN in class. I was able to analyze the data and reflect on the pedagogical implications because of the award of a summer research grant from Oakland and a summer seminar with W. Ross Winterowd, sponsored by the National Endowment for the Humanities in 1982. Furthermore, travel funds and a small development grant helped me get in touch with colleagues elsewhere who could supply criticism and suggestions. Finally, students have helped me see what needed revision, and colleagues Jerry Post and especially Louis J. Nachman have helped me with programming revisions.

I've worked on the program for about three years. My enthusiasm has grown and my knowledge has broadened each year. I am now involved with promoting CAI use at Oakland where a growing cadre of computer users is available for mutual help and support. My interest has also expanded from prewriting to include the use of computer programs throughout the writing process. Ironically, my work with the newest technology of learning has led me back to one of the oldest: I'm currently finishing a book about computers in composition.

References

Britton, J., T. Burgess, N. Martin, A. McLoed, and H. Rosen. 1975. *The development of writing abilities (11–18)*. London: Macmillan Education.

Burns, H. L., and G. H. Culp. 1980. Stimulating invention in English composition through computer-assisted instruction. *Educational Technology* 20(August): 5–10.

Dillon, G. L. 1981. *Constructing texts*. Bloomington: Indiana University Press.

Emig, J. A. 1971. *The composing processes of twelfth graders*. National Council of Teachers of English Research Report no. 13. Urbana, Ill.: NCTE.

Ford, N. 1981. Recent approaches to the study and teaching of "effective learning" in higher education. *Review of Educational Research* 51: 345–77.

Kroll, B. M. 1978. Cognitive egocentrism and the problem of audience awareness in written discourse. *Research in the Teaching of English* 12: 269–81.

Moffett, J. 1968. *Teaching the universe of discourse*. Boston: Houghton Mifflin.

Nold, E. W. 1975. Fear and trembling: The humanist approaches the computer. *College Composition and Communication* 26: 269–73.

Perkins, D. N. 1981. *The mind's best work*. Cambridge: Harvard University Press.

Rosenblatt, L. M. 1938. *Literature as exploration*. New York: D. Appleton-Century.

Schwartz, H. J. 1982. Monsters and mentors: Computer applications for humanistic education. *College English* 44: 141–52.

Smith, F. 1982. *Writing and the writer*. New York: Holt.

Winterowd, W. R. 1975. *The contemporary writer.* New York: Harcourt.
Young, R. E. 1978. Paradigms and problems: Needed research in rhetorical invention. In *Research on composing: Points of departure,* ed. C. R. Cooper and L. Odell. Urbana, Ill.: National Council of Teachers of English.

System Requirements

SEEN requires an Apple II Plus or IIe, with at least 48K RAM, 3.3 DOS, one or two disk drives, and a printer.

Program Availability

The character analysis version of SEEN can be obtained by writing Helen J. Schwartz, P.O. Box 911, Rochester, Michigan 48063.

II Editing and Grammar Programs

The three chapters in this section describe how computer programs can help edit student essays and give students basic tutoring in grammar and mechanics. Kate Kiefer and Charles Smith report in Chapter 4 on Colorado State University's use of the Writer's Workbench programs developed by Bell Laboratories. These programs help students find errors and analyze their own writing style. Chapter 5 describes HOMER, a program created by Richard Lanham and Michael Cohen for use by writing students at UCLA. HOMER is especially adept at finding elements of style that lead to "bureaucratic" writing. In Chapter 6 Michael Southwell describes how computers can be used to help students learn the basic rules of grammar.

4 Improving Students' Revising and Editing: The Writer's Workbench System

Kathleen Kiefer
Charles R. Smith
Colorado State University

As writing teachers we must teach students not only how to generate ideas but also how to create a readable product. Although we concern ourselves in our classes with both process and product, our concern with product can have unfortunate results. Approaches to teaching revision and editing often have limited success: simple drill on mechanical error always has less effect on students' writing than hoped for, and research suggests that grammar taught as grammar has no effect on the ability to write.

Confronting this concern for both process and product, we considered a computer project at Colorado State University to encourage students to revise and edit thoroughly and accurately. Such a project seemed promising. Wouldn't the objectivity of a computer encourage students to adopt a more critical stance toward their writing? Wouldn't students learn more by considering surface weaknesses in their own work rather than in the manufactured exercises of texts and handouts? Wouldn't a computer's objective analysis of patterns in diction and style result in more informed and more thorough stylistic revision? And finally, wouldn't computer assistance make possible better writing in disciplines across the campus—where all too often the term paper and other writing assignments have nearly disappeared?

The Writer's Workbench

Our project began when Charles Smith saw a word processor with a spelling checker. If spelling checkers were becoming commonplace, why weren't programs checking diction, style, and perhaps grammar? As the many spelling programs now available suggest, computers need no artificial intelligence to look for patterns—whether of spelling, diction, or style. Our search in composition journals and other standard sources showed that no one in the field had tested such programs, however. Fortunately, we chanced upon the then little-known, and little-publicized programs made at Bell Laboratories, the UNIX Writer's Workbench software.[1] Using or adapting state-of-the-art software rather than starting afresh promised to make computer-assisted editing an immediate reality in our composition classes, not a long-range goal. And so, with the full support of Rosemary Whitaker, our department head, and of Thomas McCall, head of Systems and Software at the CSU Computer Center, we approached Bell Laboratories in early summer 1981 with a plan to test the Workbench in the composition program at CSU.[2]

As negotiations for a research exchange between CSU and Bell Laboratories continued, the university funded the department's request for an Onyx 16-bit microcomputer, with word processing software from Interactive Systems Corporation, and two Perkin-Elmer 1251-I terminals. The Onyx runs UNIX, Bell Laboratories' operating system, a prerequisite for use of the Workbench. This computer can support as many as eight users simultaneously, and the Perkin-Elmer terminals have 32 special function keys for word processing, keys that make formatting and text editing simple and easy. At the same time, we leased the programs Bell made available in 1978—STYLE, DICTION, and SUGGEST. (A fourth program, SPELL, is included with the UNIX operating system.) By September 1981 we were prepared to test these four programs in two experimental sections of college composition.

Our first tests of the four Bell programs showed that students improved dramatically with even limited exposure to editing programs. On tests of editing skills, students using the four programs outperformed students in control sections by 64 percent on items covered by the Workbench, even though experimental and control classes touched on the same material in class (Kiefer and Smith 1983). On the basis of these encouraging results—and because by November we had concluded an agreement with Bell Labs to test the entire Workbench—the university committed money to expand the pilot project to six terminals and 138 students in the spring semester.

We could not use the Workbench programs in exactly the format provided by Bell Labs, however, since they were designed specifically for use at Bell. Bell users choose which programs to run on a given memo, report, or manual. Each program runs independently—to the user's eye—of other programs. Moreover, users at Bell edit on-line and run the programs interactively. We quickly discovered that students using just four programs needed much more time than we could accommodate if they followed this pattern and made thorough revisions at the terminal. Some of the programs, too, were less useful for students than for the writers at Bell Laboratories: our students rarely use acronyms, for instance, and if they use sexist language, it falls into limited patterns unlike the job titles Bell highlights in its SEXIST diction program. Finally, we wanted to guarantee that students would use all beneficial programs, not run them haphazardly.

We selected the 17 Workbench programs and program parts we wanted students to consider on every paper, and Blake Stewart, an analyst in the CSU Computer Center, designed additions to the UNIX shell program so that students could give only one command and receive within minutes both their papers and program results at the printer. Other tailoring of the Workbench required little expert programming. The Workbench DICTION program, for example, allows users to select items for flagging and to except others. Users also set standards based on typical documents or papers. Most of our refinements, then, entailed selecting appropriate programs, revising dictionaries, and setting reasonable standards for the papers in college composition.

The Program in Action

Since spring 1982 the project has expanded to include the entire composition program of 4,000 students per year using 27 terminals and four Onyx computers. Students bring written rough drafts of their essays to the terminal room, type the essays into the computer, making whatever revisions they wish as they type, run the SPELL program interactively to reduce spelling and typographical errors, and then call for the programs to print results. Students collect the output, take it home for consideration and revision, return to the terminal room to enter changes, and then call for a clean copy of the text to submit for grading. Should teachers require another revision after grading, the computer copy of the paper is available for about three weeks after the student last changed the essay.

The following is a sample of program results based on a student paper.[3] The first program, ORGANIZATION, prints only the first and last sentence of each paragraph; the third program shown here prints the entire paper. In the SUGGEST program reference is made to GLOSSARY. This is a handout students receive the first day of class.

```
      * * * ORGANIZATION * * *
  Maybe You Shouldn't Go Away to College.
Going away to college is not for
everyone. Money, finding stabiltiy while
```

changes are occurring, and accepting
responsibility are three to consider.

Money is likely to be most important.
Whether room and board is a dorm or an
apartment, the expense is great.

Most students never stop to consider
that the money that could be saved from
room and board may be better spent in
the future years on graduate school,
which is likely to be more impor5ant in
their careers.

Going to school is a time of many
changes anyway, without adding the
pressure of a new city or even a new
state. Starting to college could be an
emotional time for some, and the
security of their home and faimily might
make everything easier.

When students decide to go away to
school, sometimes because their friends
are going away, or maybe because the
school is their parents' alma mater,
something they all need to decide is
whether or not they can accept the
responsibility of a completely new way
of life.

Everyone feels as if they are ready for
total independence when they decide to
go away to college, but is breaking away
when they are just beginning to set
their futures a good idea?

Going away to school may be the right
road for some, but those who feel that

they are not ready might start looking
to a future that is just around the
cornor.

* * * DEVELOPMENT * * *
A survey of twenty-five essays shows the
following averages: introductions, 120
words; body paragraphs, 180 words; and
conclusions, 100 words. An effective
introduction, conclusion, or body
paragraph may be of any length, but a
typical weakness of paragraphs is
insufficient development.*

Since your introduction is considerably
shorter than average, please check to be
sure it introduces the essay gracefully.

Similarly, some of your body paragraphs
are much shorter than average. Please
check paragraphs 2, 3, 4, 5, and 6 for
lack of development.

Your conclusion, too, is considerably
shorter than average; please check to be
sure you've released, not dropped, the
reader.

*NOTE: Quotations set apart from the
text may render some or all of the
information in DEVELOPMENT inaccurate.

* * * DICTION AND TO BE VERBS * * *
(MAYBE) You Shouldn't Go Away To
College. Going away to college IS not
for everyone. *(THERE ARE)* good
reasons why a student might choose to
live at home and attend a local school.
Money, finding stabiltiy while changes

ARE occurring, and accepting
responsibility ARE three to consider.

Money IS likely to BE most important.
Not only IS tuition more expensive, but
extra money IS needed for room and
board. Whether room and board IS a dorm
or an apartment, the expense IS great.

Most students never stop to consider
that the money that could BE saved from
room and board may BE better spent in
the future years on graduate school,
which IS likely to BE more impor5ant in
their careers.

Going to school IS a time of many
changes anyway, without adding the
pressure of a new city or even a new
state. Finding stability will behard
enough, without going from home to a
dorm. Starting to college could BE an
emotional time for some, and the
security of their home and faimily might
make everything easier.

When students decide to go away to
school, sometimes because their friends
ARE going away, or *(MAYBE)* because
the school is their parents' alma mater,
something they all need to decide IS
(WHETHER OR NOT) they can accept the
responsibility of a completely new way
of life.

Everyone feels as if they ARE ready for
total independence when they decide to
go away to college, but IS breaking away
when they ARE just beginning to set
their futures a good idea?

Going away to school may <u>BE</u> the right
road for some, but those who feel that
they <u>ARE</u> not ready might start looking
to a future that <u>IS</u> just around the
cornor.

　　　　　＊ ＊ ＊ SUGGEST ＊ ＊ ＊
maybe: use ''GLOSSARY'' for ''maybe''
there are: use ''GLOSSARY'' for ''there
are.''
whether or not: use ''whether'' for
''whether or not''

　＊ Some suggestions will be
inappropriate for your context.＊

　＊＊ When several suggestions appear for
a single word or phrase flagged, choose
appropriately.＊＊

　　　　　＊ ＊ ＊ VAGUENESS INDEX ＊ ＊ ＊
In this text, 9.6 percent of the words
are vague.

Below is a list of the vague words in
your text. Delete where possible.
Otherwise, replace or supplement with
specific words, phrases, or examples so
that your index is as low as possible,
preferably below 3%.

you	everything	great
most	some	going
more	going	going
make	more	responsibility
going	many	most
go	go	some
important	good	something
going		

```
          * * * SPELLING * * *
Possible spelling errors in college are:

behard         cornor       dorm
faimily        impor5ant    stabiltiy

          * * * CHECK * * *
accept except  accept: ''take''; except:
''other than, exclude''
choose chose  choose: ''to select'';
chose: past tense of ''choose''
everyone everybody: requires singular,
not plural (their, they) as referent
most: check GLOSSARY when you could
substitute **ALMOST**
sit sat set  sit,sat: ''to be seated'';
set: ''to place, put down''

          * * * PUNCTUATION * * *
A description of the punctuation in
college.

0 double quotes and 0 single quotes
1 apostrophe
0 left parentheses and 0 right ones

Sentences probably incorrectly
punctuated followed by correction:

No errors found in college.

          * * * GRAMMAR * * *
For file college:

No split infinitives found

          * * * PROSE * * *
BECAUSE YOUR TEXT IS SHORT ( <2000 WORDS
```

& <100 SENTENCES), THE FOLLOWING
ANALYSIS MAY BE MISLEADING.

PROSE compares your text to twenty or
more similar texts written for the
course you are taking and classified as
good by several teachers of that course.

READABILITY
The Kincaid readability formula predicts
that your text can be read by someone
with 11 or more years of schooling, a
good score for texts in this course.

VARIATION
You have an appropriate distribution of
sentence types.

SENTENCE STRUCTURE
Passives
This text contains 13.0% passive voice.

Good papers in CO150 typically contain
fewer than 5%. Check each sentence below
for effective use of the passive, and
convert all ineffective passives to
active. For help, see p. 15 in your
Manual.

Not only is *tuition* more expensive,
but extra money is needed for room and
board.

Most students never stop to consider
that the money that could be saved from
room and board may be better spent in
the future years on graduate school,
which is likely to be more impor5ant in
their careers.

STYLE summarizes information from sentence and word counts. Here students check the balance of long and short sentences, the balance of simple and complex sentences, the percentage of *to be* verbs, and the percentage of subject openers. Finally, the ABSTRACT program informs students when the percent of abstract words in the essay suggests that more specific detail and examples may be necessary. (For more information on the Workbench program components, see the list under Program Availability at the end of this chapter.)

Student Response

While students often need help interpreting Workbench output on early papers, we have found most students quick to learn to use the programs. Typically, our students write two short papers at the beginning of the semester so that most of the early suggestions concern the use of *to be* verbs and diction. In a short time, students are able to move to STYLE and PROSE for help with more complex revisions, to VAGUENESS and ABSTRACT for help with specific diction and support. Most important, as students begin making general use of the programs, they learn that the greatest value of Workbench lies in its ability to raise questions, to help with revision and reconsideration—not merely to point out error.

In all classes queried about attitudes toward computer-assisted editing, students have responded positively, often enthusiastically. Without fail, students in experimental groups feel that CAI does not damage student-teacher relationships (shift from unsure response to positive response significant at $p < .01$ in all tests).[4] In addition, students enjoy using the computer to prepare papers. In the first pilot project with 140 students using the full Workbench, 76 percent of the students agreed that using the computer added to their enjoyment of the course; 86 percent felt that the computer was easy to learn to use; 73 percent felt that the computer printouts were not too detailed; 63 percent felt that they were learning more about style and diction than if they had no computer assistance; and, astonishingly, 65 percent agreed that "if the next composition course I take uses computers, I will look forward to it." Even two years into the project, when the novelty has worn off a bit, students continue to react positively.

As we have expanded the project to include groups other than composition students, we have seen similarly positive responses to the word processor and editing programs. Of 247 students in basic composition in fall 1982, 61 percent enjoyed using the computer, 58 percent found it easy to learn to use (and fewer of these students type), 65 percent found the printouts appropriately detailed, and 49 percent felt they were learning more about style and diction. Only 48 percent looked forward to another composition class, but perhaps fewer respond positively here because they know they have another composition class to take at CSU.

Of students in two advanced writing courses, 65 percent enjoy using the computer, 80 percent find it easy to learn, 75 percent would look forward to another class, and 70 percent approve of the detail included on the printouts. In this group only half felt they were learning more about style and diction.

But attitudes alone are not the proof of a computer project. Students in college composition consistently improve 40 to 50 percent more on tests of editing skill than do counterparts in control groups, even when the same teacher follows the same syllabus in each of two semesters, one with a control group and one with an experimental group (see Frase et al., forthcoming).

We have not, however, completed all the testing we hope to do of improvement in students' writing and editing skills. One early test showed slight gain in students' ability to write impromptu essays after using the Workbench for a semester; we need to repeat that test to determine exactly how the Workbench or use of a text editor changes students' performance on impromptu writing assignments. We also hope to gauge the long-term effects of the Workbench by studying students who use such aids throughout their college experience.

Using the computer as we have has not changed contact hours for writing courses with computer assistance. Students still meet for the same number of hours a week with instructors and schedule computer time outside regular class meetings. But most teachers are now using the Workbench in classroom activities so that the course syllabi have changed somewhat since we began the computer project. Some teachers, having run a peer review on the written rough drafts of essays, may ask students to bring Workbench output to a special editing workshop devoted to a common problem the class is having with the program results or with a particular point of style. Such workshops may last ten minutes or the entire class as students help each other interpret results, recast sentences, revise paragraphs, and improve the essay. We have found this approach to be one of the most successful for helping students learn to evaluate the output more quickly. Other teachers take different approaches to the editing aids. Several of our graduate teaching assistants, for instance, ask students to bring the printed output for the first peer review. The teachers focus their questions on organization, development, and effectiveness of the argument and ask students to consider stylistic matters as they feel necessary given the output. Still other teachers prepare students to use the output wisely by bringing exercises that show the advantages and disadvantages of taking the results literally. These teachers select exercises that supplement their other classroom activities; for instance, one teacher brings an exercise on vague language when he discusses vivid description and then asks for student samples of vivid language when students write their own descriptive papers.

Instructor Response

In 1982–83, nearly the entire composition program—including 30 English Department faculty members and 30 graduate teaching assistants—used the programs in six different writing courses. Surveys of these 60 instructors and their varied approaches to composition also attest to the value of the Workbench. In the pilot project, the six selected teachers were uniformly pleased with the improved papers they received. Most agreed that students had a more positive attitude toward college composition now that they used the computer to prepare papers. All teachers agreed that the Workbench emphasized style and diction appropriately for the class, and all agreed that students felt comfortable using the Workbench suggestions. Most agreed that the Workbench did not save them time in grading. When we followed up on that response, we discovered, however, that teachers spent a larger portion of their evaluation time commenting on structure and logic rather than editing. The few who spent more time grading felt they invested their time in more fruitful comment.

When we polled all instructors using the computer programs in fall 1982—ten faculty members and 18 graduate assistants responded—we saw much the same result. Most agreed that the computer programs reinforced their grading practices because the student who had not revised for wordiness, for instance, saw similar comments from the computer and the instructor. Most agreed that grading was not speeded, but that papers were cleaner. Most also agreed that the uniform format of all papers eased grading, that the computer programs sensitize students to highlighted errors or weaknesses, and that style and diction are appropriately emphasized. Results from the spring semester surveys are similarly positive.

Conclusion

Through June 1983, we supported the project by charging a course fee of $15 per student. In fall 1983, with the university decision to support computing on campus through a slight tuition increase, we planned to expand the project to 44 terminals and a larger computer. Because of the expanded capacity, our textual analysis center will be open to all students doing writing assignments for course work anywhere on campus—with the proviso that the instructor devote some time and attention to writing problems. Instructors will thus be able to refer individual students and entire classes to our computer room for help with writing. With our expanded capacity we hope, too, to take advantage of recent work on prewriting programs to aid our basic writers and others who need help brainstorming and narrowing. In addition to continuing our tests of the Workbench, we hope to develop specifications for additional programs, especially those encouraging students to revise still more and to edit for more serious grammatical weaknesses. Though we do not expect to have the capacity to allow students to compose on our terminals, we hope that developments in computer networking will allow students to bring electronic files to our central facility for access to the Workbench. In short, computers and Bell Laboratories' Workbench promise to continue to help us improve the quality of writing at CSU.

Notes

1. UNIX is a trademark of AT&T Bell Laboratories.
2. Patricia Gingrich acted as our liaison with Bell Laboratories and provided valuable advice and technical assistance.
3. Our thanks to Jean Wyrick and Holt, Rinehart and Winston for permission to use a student essay from *Steps to Writing Well* (1979).
4. Our thanks to Doug Sjogren, professor of Education, who helped with statistical analysis, and to the teachers of experimental and control sections— Carolyn Duff, James Garvey, William McBride, Carol Mitchell, David Mogen, Edward Schamberger, Karen Schneider, and Ward Swinson.

References

Frase, L. T., K. E. Kiefer, and C. R. Smith. Forthcoming. Theory and practice of computer-aided instruction. In *Evaluation, response, and revision,* ed. S. Freedman.

Kiefer, K. E., and C. R. Smith. 1983. Textual analysis with computers: Tests of Bell Laboratories' computer software. *Research in the Teaching of English* 17: 201–14.

Smith, C. R., and K. E. Kiefer. 1983. Using the Writer's Workbench programs at Colorado State University. *Sixth international conference on computers and the humanities,* ed. S. K. Burton and D. D. Short. Rockville, Md.: Computer Science Press.

A Brief Bibliography on the Writer's Workbench

Cherry, L. L. 1981. Computer aids for writers. *ACM Sigplan Notices* 16, no. 6 (June): 62–67.

———. 1982. Writing tools. *IEEE Transactions on Communications* 30, no. 1 (January): 100–105.

Cherry, L. L., and W. Vesterman. 1981. *Writing tools—The STYLE and DICTION programs.* Computing Science Technical Report, no. 91. Murray Hill, N. J.: Bell Laboratories. (Available on request.)

Cherry, L. L., et al. 1983. UNIX Writer's Workbench software: Computer aids for text analysis. *Bell Laboratories Record,* May/June, 10–16.

Frase, L. T. 1983. Writer's Workbench: Philosophy. *The Bell System Technical Journal,* pt. 3, July/Aug.

Frase, L. T., et al. 1981. Computer aids for text assessment and writing instruction. *NSPI Journal,* Nov. 21–24.

Gingrich, P. S. 1983. Writer's Workbench: Results of a field study. *The Bell System Technical Journal,* pt. 3, July/Aug.

Heidorn, G. E., et al. 1982. The EPISTLE text-critiquing system. *IBM Systems Journal* 21: 305–27.

Macdonald, N. H. 1983. Writer's Workbench: Rationale and design. *The Bell System Technical Journal,* pt. 3, July/August.

Macdonald, N. H., et al. 1982. The Writer's Workbench: Computer aids for text analysis. *IEEE Transactions on Communications* 30, no. 1 (January): 105–10.

Miller, L. A., et al. 1981. Text-critiquing with the EPISTLE system: An author's aid to better syntax. In *Proceedings of the National Computer Conference,* 649–55. Arlington, Va.: AFIPS Press.

Smith, C. R., and K. E. Kiefer. 1982. Computer-assisted editing in expository writing. In *Proceedings of the Second Annual Role of Computer in Education Conference,* 87–90. Joint publication of MICRO-IDEAS, Glenview, Ill., and William Rainey Harper College, Palatine, Ill.

System Requirements

The Writer's Workbench will run on any computer with the UNIX operating system.

Program Availability

UNIX Writer's Workbench software is available from AT&T Technologies. The Workbench programs in use at Colorado State University are as follows:

> ORGANIZATION prints the first and last sentence of each paragraph to give the writer an abstract or outline of an essay. Students can use the output as a check for focus, unity, and coherence.

DEVELOPMENT counts words in each paragraph and compares those figures with averages drawn from sample papers for the course; if the figures are significantly lower than the averages, the program reminds students that paragraphs can be any length but suggests writers check for adequate detail.

FINDBE capitalizes and underlines all forms of *to be* appearing in students' texts. Students check for weak expletive and passive constructions and revise for active verb choice as necessary.

DICTION highlights (i.e., capitalizes and encloses in brackets) any of about 500 wordy, overused, misused, sexist, and inflated words and phrases.

SUGGEST follows the text with possible substitutions for words and phrases highlighted by DICTION. SUGGEST cautions students to choose wisely because the program cannot evaluate the context for substitution.

VAGUENESS INDEX flags any of 140 vague or general words. If the text has more than 5 percent of these words, the printout lists them and recommends revisions; if the text has less than 5 percent, students see only the percentage.

SPELL lists typographical and spelling errors.

CHECK lists commonly confused homophones and word pairs when the writer has used one of the words in the text. The program includes a brief distinction between the two words or a reference to the glossary (a handout all students receive the first day of class) for longer explanations.

PUNCTUATION checks for missing parentheses and for patterns of punctuation—periods followed by capital letters, commas and periods inside quotation marks, semicolons and colons outside quotation marks, periods inside parentheses for complete sentences, and so on. It lists both the sentence as punctuated in the student's paper and a suggested change.

GRAMMAR identifies most split infinitives and misuses of *a* and *an*.

PROSE compares values for ten stylistic criteria in a student's paper with standards derived from the best papers written for that course. When the student's value falls outside a range of $\pm$ one standard deviation from the mean, the program suggests improvements.

PASSIVE prints out all passive sentences appearing in a student's text with a reminder to use only effective passive constructions and to change ineffective passives to active voice.

NOMINALIZATION prints out all sentences with nominalized words (nouns ending in *-ance*, *-ence*, *-ion*, or *-ment*) when the percentage of nominalizations exceeds 3 percent of the total number of words.

STYLE summarizes information about sentence length, type, and sentence opening and word class counts.

ABSTRACT compares words in a text to a dictionary of 314 abstract words (determined through psycholinguistic research). If students use more than 2.3 percent of these words in a text, the program prints a message reminding students to check for adequate concrete detail.

5 HOMER: Teaching Style with a Microcomputer

Michael E. Cohen
Richard A. Lanham
University of California, Los Angeles

Computers deal only in discrete phenomena; they follow rigid procedures to manipulate and transform precise data. Can these machines help teach something as complex and subjective as writing style? Can Melissa run her essay, "My Opinion of Life," on a 6502B microprocessor and hope for some reasonable stylistic advice?

It depends on what we mean by "reasonable stylistic advice." We don't expect (or, at least, we shouldn't soon expect) machines to judge whether or not a student has used irony effectively or whether an essay's prose is more lyrical than the topic requires. No one yet has successfully quantified irony or lyricism, and what we haven't quantified, computers can't calculate.

So we must give ourselves and our machines more limited goals. While not pretending to quantify all that the word *style* comprises, we can describe some few of its more rudimentary components. *Revising Prose,* written by Richard Lanham and published by Scribner's in 1979, discusses some of these simple, easily ascertainable stylistic features, and it presents a simple, precise, mechanical method for finding and evaluating them. The HOMER program, released by Scribner's in 1983, automates the method that *Revising Prose* presents.

The Method

Revising Prose gives the same advice as many other style textbooks. It recommends that writers use active rather than passive verbs whenever possible, that they avoid needlessly abstract language, that they shun wordiness. Sound advice, though limited. Unlike many books, however, *Revising Prose* explicitly recognizes those limits. It does not pretend to tackle all stylistic problems but only a small range of them. Above all, it gives student writers some manageable first steps to take when revising.

The book describes an "Official Style," a style that bureaucrats, academicians, politicians, journalists—and students—employ all too frequently. A preponderance of prepositional phrases, passive verbs, noun phrases, and lengthy, shapeless sentences characterizes the Official Style. *Revising Prose* presents a "Paramedic Method" that helps writers clear away some of the Official Style's verbal debris. It suggests, for a start, that writers perform a quick diagnosis on their texts: circle all the *be* verbs and prepositions, make a chart of sentence lengths, and temporarily ignore meaning and look at surface features. The HOMER program performs these mechanical tasks, but before we examine how the program works, we should first explore the Paramedic Method's rationale.

Why pick on prepositions? Prepositions have their uses, and no sustained piece of writing can do entirely without them. When prepositional phrases get strung together, however, readers start having problems. Each preposition creates a relationship between its object and the rest of the sentence or clause in which it appears. Stringing prepositional phrases together creates a chain of such relationships; the longer the chain, the harder the reader works to resolve all the dependent relationships. Prose that relies heavily upon such strings makes the reader work very hard indeed. Many student writers let these little words do the big job of organizing their thoughts, but ambiguities can arise and meanings may become lost.

Be verbs have their uses, too. Much like the equal sign in a mathematical statement, they assert that some thing or some relationship exists, that A *is* A. As a sentence's main verb, a *be* verb drains prose of action. As part of a passive construction, it helps conceal important facts. Consider the following sentence:

Teachers' salaries were reduced.

This sentence doesn't state *who* reduced the salaries. Instead, it merely presents the formula, "Teachers' salaries = reduced." Writers may have good reasons for not revealing who does what in their prose: those facts may have no importance or the writer may not know them or the writer may not wish them known. But, more often, writers just unthinkingly assume that the reader already knows, or can guess, who the actors are.

The formulaic verbal patterns that define the Official Style usually produce long sentences, and that only makes the reader's burden heavier. Consider what sort of prose the reader must decipher: myriad prepositional phrases tenuously connecting complicated ideas, floating in murky, overlong, actorless sentences.

The Program

The Paramedic Method draws the writer's eye to Official Style outbreaks. But circling prepositions and *be* verbs and graphing sentence lengths manually takes time and patience. Applying the method to a long text can prove unendurably tedious—and once applied, it still leaves the writer with the main job: revising. That's where HOMER comes in. HOMER does the bean counting, leaving the student writer free for the big job.

The HOMER program requires an Apple II, Apple II Plus, or Apple IIe computer equipped with the Apple Pascal operating system (UCLA students use a customized HOMER running on an IBM 3033 mainframe, but Apples cost much less than IBM 3033's). Apple Pascal provides a relatively simple text editor, and students use this when they compose their rough drafts. Although it takes students some time to learn how the text editor works, it saves them time when they revise. And a program like HOMER encourages revision.

Once students have completed their rough drafts, they save them on floppy disks. HOMER can then "read" these magnetically stored texts and analyze them. Students may choose to have the program examine their texts for as many as four different word types simultaneously: prepositions, *be* verbs, words containing *tion* or *sion* (nominalized verbs more often than not), and vague words (which HOMER calls "Woolly" words). The program keeps track of how often each word type appears in a text and also counts the total number of words and sentences.

The Paramedic Method uses visual cues as well as statistical ones; writers must know, for example, not only how many prepositions they used, but where they used them. HOMER provides two sorts of visual aids. The first is the "verbal surface map." The following sample shows a verbal surface map of this chapter's first two paragraphs.

```
Prepositions = ''P''
''To be'' verbs = ''T''
''Shun'' words = ''S''
''Woolly'' words = ''W''

Here's your map--GOOD LUCK, Anonymous!!!

Computers deal only in discrete phenomena;
- - - P - -
they follow rigid procedures to manipulate and
- - - - P - -
```

```
transform precise data.
- - -
Can these machines help teach something as
- - - - - - -
complex and subjective as writing style?
- - - - - -
Can Melissa run her essay, ''My Opinion of
- - - - - - - P
Life,'' on a 6502B microprocessor and hope
W P - - - - -
for some reasonable stylistic advice?
P - - - -
It depends on what we mean by ''reasonable
- - P - - - P -
stylistic advice.''
- -
We don't expect (or, at least, we shouldn't
- - - - P - - -
soon expect) machines to judge whether or not a
- - - P - - - - -
student has used irony effectively or whether
- - - - - - -
an essay's prose is more lyrical than the topic
- - - T - - - - -
requires.
-
No one yet has successfully quantified irony or
- - - - - - - -
lyricism, and what we haven't quantified,
- - - - - -
computers can't calculate.
- - -
```

The computer displays the text, sentence by sentence, on the left; the map appears on the right. (The map must be shown between text lines here because of the book page dimensions.) A student may regard the map as something like a high-contrast aerial photograph of the text, where ordinary words appear as hyphens, prepositions as P's, forms of *to be* as T's, and so forth. The map lets student writers see where the various word types appear, how they cluster, and how they interact.

Writers who wish a less denatured view of their texts may choose HOMER's second display technique. This technique rearranges the text so that every time HOMER finds a word that matches one of its four word types, it begins a new line, pulling that word out to the left margin. The next sample illustrates how this looks.

```
Here comes your text, Anonymous:

       Computers deal only
in  discrete phenomena; they follow rigid procedures
to  manipulate and transform precise data.
       Can these machines help teach something as complex
       and subjective as writing style?
       Can Melissa run her essay, ''My Opinion
of  Life,''
on  a 6502B microprocessor and hope
for some reasonable stylistic advice?
       It depends
on  what we mean
by  ''reasonable stylistic advice.''
       We don't expect (or,
at  least, we shouldn't soon expect) machines
to  judge whether or not a student has used irony
       effectively or whether an essay's prose is more
       lyrical than the topic requires.
       No one yet has successfully quantified irony or
       lyricism, and what we haven't quantified,
       computers can't calculate.
```

The second display tactic lets writers see the word types in context and works especially well with prepositions, as text displayed this way helps emphasize how prepositional phrases affect a sentence's rhythm.

Texts also have larger rhythmic features, and a sentence length graph may reveal something about them. If a graph shows that most sentences have nearly the same length, it may imply that the prose has a sing-song rhythm which may unintentionally lull readers to sleep. Here, variety is the spice of life; it helps break the monotony. The sample Sentence Length graph measures the six sentences of this chapter's first two paragraphs.

```
=x=x=x=x==x=x=x=x=x Sentence Length
x=x=x=x=x==x=x=x=x=

    +   10   +   20   +   30   +   40   +   50   +   60

###################
##################
#########################
############
###########################################
#####################
```

After HOMER presents the mapped text, it produces a statistical summary. The statistics always include a word count, sentence count, and sentence length. The program may also produce a comment if the average sentence length is too long or too short. HOMER provides statistics as well for each word type the user has chosen and may again produce written comments. Here is a sample statistical summary:

```
                    STATISTICS
Number of words:
   110
Number of sentences:
   6
Average words per sentence:
   18.33

Number of prepositions:
   9
Average prepositions per sentence:
   1.50
Word to preposition ratio:
   12.22
4 sentences contained prepositions
You keep your PREPOSITIONS under
control--how admirable!

Number of ''to be'' verbs:
   1
Average ''to be'' verbs per sentence:
   0.17
Word to ''to be'' verb ratio:
   110.00
1 sentence contained ''to be'' verbs
I see you avoid ''to be'' verbs--how
delightful!!

Number of ''shun'' words:
   0
Average ''shun'' words per sentence:
   0.00
```

```
Word to ''shun'' word ratio:
   110.00
Good work--few ''shun'' words often
means clearer writing!!

Number of ''woolly'' words:
   1
Average ''woolly'' words per sentence:
   0.17
Word to ''woolly'' word ratio:
   110.00
1 sentence contained ''woolly'' words
I'm glad you haven't pulled the
''woolly'' words over my eyes.
```

The statistical summary presents yet another view of a student's prose—a numerical one. It as little reflects a text's meaning or value as age, weight, or IQ reflects a person's character. The summary, at best, reflects gross stylistic tendencies, nothing more.

The comments that HOMER makes explicate the statistics. The comments also, by their rather offbeat tone, implicitly emphasize that the statistics don't present a complete picture. Statistics have an illusory authority, one that students should not trust blindly: the Gettysburg Address and a bureaucrat's job description might produce very similar statistics, but that hardly means the two pieces share any other qualities. While a HOMER comment like

```
OH MY! All these ''TO BE'' VERBS
distress me!!
```

may help a student make sense of the numbers, it also stresses that the program's interpretation is an opinion—and not a wholly trustworthy one. (Teachers may modify the program's comments and the statistical averages that trigger them, but they can't suppress the program's personality completely.)

Conclusion

Can HOMER help students write better? We return to our original question: Can a machine help teach something as complex and subjective as writing style? The answer is yes—for some students, sometimes. A student who writes Official Stylese may, with HOMER's aid, see prose through new eyes, while a student who has more severe writing problems may find HOMER's analysis totally irrelevant. Whether or not HOMER does any good depends, finally, on the teacher. A machine can *help* teach style, but only a teacher can decide when and how to use the machine.

System Requirements

HOMER runs on Apple II computers with 64K RAM, two disk drives, and the Apple Pascal operating system (available from most Apple dealers).

Program Availability

HOMER is sold by Charles Scribner's Sons.

6 The COMP-LAB Writing Modules: Computer-Assisted Grammar Instruction

Michael G. Southwell
York College

Bork (1980) has suggested that in the near future most instruction will take place with the help of computers. Presenting instruction is already an important use of computers in higher education (Magarell 1983), and a recent survey showed it to be of high interest to teachers of writing (Janello 1983). I describe in this chapter an effort to exploit the potential of computers for providing instruction in grammar to students whose writing exhibits severe problems of correctness and clarity. These basic writing students are usually members of various ethnic minorities, and their writing problems are typically associated with some sort of non-standard speech background. My colleagues and I have accumulated evidence that intensive and systematic instruction in grammar can improve not only the correctness but also the overall quality of such students' writing. (We hope soon to publish this evidence.)

The COMP-LAB Writing Modules are a set of computer lessons for these students. They are designed to provide instruction in the grammar of standard English and are currently being used at York College. The modules are based on autotutorial written exercises developed by Carolyn Kirkpatrick, Mary Epes, and me for use in the COMP-LAB, York's autotutorial writing laboratory. These lab exercises are available, in workbook format, as *The COMP-LAB Exercises,* a textbook published by Prentice-Hall in 1980. When complete, the CAI modules will offer instruction in five of the grammatical features that most commonly cause problems for basic writing students:

Noun plural forms

Verbs and subjects

Verb agreement

Past-tense verb forms

To be verbs

Design

The COMP-LAB Writing Modules assume that the best strategy for helping basic writing students overcome their writing problems is not to try to get them to correct individual, isolated mistakes, but rather to have them learn standard written English as if it were an entirely new language (Epes, Kirkpatrick, and Southwell 1979). The modules thus have much more in common with English as a Second Language instruction than with traditional English grammar instruction. That is, they are developmental rather than remedial: they aim at creating understanding of a language system rather than at fixing incorrect features in isolation.

Pedagogical Design

The modules follow what my colleagues and I believe are the best principles for developmental instruction. Instead of trying to teach everything, the modules are highly selective: they deal only with noun and verb forms. Errors in these features are both pervasive in the writing of these students and highly stigmatizing. Limiting the instruction allows the modules to reinforce each other and lessens the chance that students will become confused by a variety of problems, some much less important than others.

Second, the modules make no assumptions about students' knowledge of grammar. The modules teach every important principle so that students are never faced with a task they haven't been prepared for. Third, instruction is broken into manageable portions. Students are asked to do many things but only one new thing at a time, a procedure that improves their chances of mastering each successive task. Presenting instruction in bits is the best way to help students assemble a thorough understanding of a complex and interrelated system like written English.

Fourth, the modules are incremental. Each module, though independent, builds on previous ones. Even as students are learning what they will need for the harder lessons to come, they are reviewing previous learning. Recapitulation of earlier lessons reinforces students' knowledge, and lets them experience frequent success.

Finally, the modules provide extensive practice in contexts. It's easy to program computers to evaluate short answers, but it has often been observed that students usually can't transfer success at this kind of exercise to their own writing. Learning to use forms in the isolated contexts of exercises doesn't help when what is needed is control of forms in the context of extended discourse. And so the modules permit or, where appropriate, require students to use forms in the context of whole sentences and, to a limited extent, paragraphs. This activity is much closer to writing actual papers than the filling in of blanks or the even more useless choosing from a list of alternatives.

The Special Strengths of CAI

Computers can enhance the effectiveness of instruction in at least three ways, each of which is exploited in the COMP-LAB modules. First, they offer an efficient way to manage students' use of lessons. COMP-LAB users work on a predetermined sequence of lessons. A series of menus helps students orient themselves by reminding them where they are in the sequence. Passwords (given at the end of one lesson and requested at the beginning of the next) make it difficult for students to skip lessons or to do them out of order. Although it has sometimes been argued that learners should control their instruction, there is evidence that programmed control is just as effective, especially in a computer environment (Lahey 1979). Developmental students in particular benefit from a structured rather than an open environment.

Second, computers offer many possibilities for presentation of instructional materials. Selective on-screen erasing and writing can be used to focus students' attention on the most important concept, as can highlighting and blinking of text. The computer controls the speed of presentation, displaying text in conceptually logical chunks and delaying or slowing it for emphasis. Colors can be used to highlight text, to emphasize a concept (by, for example, distinguishing between a base form of a word and its inflected form), and to provide warnings or reinforce messages. Sound can be used in many of the same ways and is particularly useful as a prompt, reminding students that the computer is waiting for them to do something. Good quality software-based speech synthesis is now possible. It is used in the modules to help students hear the sounds of the endings they are learning to employ in writing. Movable graphics objects are used in the modules both to emphasize the meaning of the text, when appropriate, and to shift instruction into a mode closer to that of play. There is powerful evidence that play- and gamelike activities can increase the power of instruction (Allen, Allen, and Ross 1970; Malone 1980).

Third, computers provide powerful autotutorial instruction. My colleagues and I have discussed elsewhere the virtues (and limitations) of autotutorial instruction in writing (Kirkpatrick 1981; Epes, Kirkpatrick, and Southwell 1982) and the particular power that computers bring to an autotutorial mode (Southwell 1982a). Autotutorial instruction clearly allocates responsibility for learning to the learner; students who are working by themselves at a computer understand quickly that the responsibility for the learning is theirs alone. Computer-assisted instruction, which is not dependent on the presence of a teacher or even a tutor, also increases students' motivation. Able to work when they want and at their own pace, students are more likely to do the work. The computer's ability to adapt the sequence of instructional materials on the basis of students' responses makes it possible for students to receive instruction that is truly individualized. One student understands a concept quickly, and the computer sends her or him on without further delay; another student needs additional explanation and practice, and the computer patiently provides it until he or she is ready to move on; a third student needs to review prior instruction, and the computer sends this student back to an earlier lesson. Moreover, the computer's interactivity keeps students involved in their learning; instead of passively reading or listening, they are actively engaged in manipulating or responding to a text. There is no doubt that learning is enhanced by this kind of involvement (see, for example, Piaget 1954). And precisely because it is interactive, the computer can provide students with the immediate feedback that accelerates learning. Exercises are not secret tests; mistakes are not simple failures but become opportunities for further learning, with instruction aimed directly at the kind of misunderstandings students have exhibited.

Description of the Modules

The COMP-LAB Writing Modules are available on microcomputers in York's autotutorial writing lab, which is open all day every weekday. They are used on a drop-in basis by a range of students, from those enrolled in intermediate English as a Second Language courses to seniors preparing for York's Proficiency Examination. The majority of users, though, are students in York's basic writing course, who do the exercises as part of their required lab work. Since the lessons are available at any time, students go to the lab whenever it's convenient for them to work on their assignments. Students are not graded directly on their lab work; rather, this instruction is intended to improve the writing they do for the course. And because teachers are freed from much of the burden of teaching grammar, a larger proportion of their limited classroom time can be devoted to instruction in rhetoric and composing skills. Just as important, separating these two kinds of instruction and actually presenting them in two different locations helps students to understand each better (Epes, Kirkpatrick, and Southwell 1979; Winterowd, 1980) and thus is likely to foster better writing. (Further details on the use of the CAI lessons may be found in Southwell [1982b, 1983].)

At the moment, approximately six hours of computer-assisted instruction are available in a time-sharing format and about three hours in the microcomputer format I will describe here. The quantity of instruction is too limited to have a measurable impact on students' writing, so no attempt has been made to evaluate the specific effect of the CAI lessons. But there is ample evidence (based on questionnaires and informal interviews) that students enjoy working at the computer and appreciate the lessons. Perhaps the most striking evidence is that students do the lessons and even ask for more. Since basic writing students are typically impatient with, and unsuccessful at, conventional instruction, this seems to me to be clear evidence that they perceive the CAI lessons as beneficial.

Contents

Each module consists of from five to seven integrated lessons. A description of the Verb Agreement module will give some sense of the contents of a typical module. The module consists of six lessons:

Lesson 1: Using the computer

Lesson 2: Identifying verbs

Lesson 3: Identifying subjects

Lesson 4: Plural subjects

Lesson 5: Singular subjects

Lesson 6: Special problems

Lesson 1 is an introduction to the computer and its keyboard. This lesson is offered to students at the beginning of every module. Students learn the locations of the various keys and the use of special function keys such as CONTROL, ESCAPE, BREAK, and RETURN. They are reminded that they must differentiate between letters and numbers, and they learn the protocols of typing on the computer: locating themselves on the screen with the cursor, typing with text wraparound, and responding to prompts. This kind of acclimatizing is particularly important for basic writing students, who sometimes do not know how to type and who are insecure when faced with unfamiliar kinds of instruction. But students quickly become familiar with the computer.

Lesson 2 helps students to learn what verbs are and to identify them. After trying out some faulty definitions, students learn a reliable one based on linguistic theory: that a verb is the word that changes when the tense is changed. Later in the lesson, they work at memorizing the rule and practice using it to find verbs in sentences. The following sample shows how students must demonstrate their understanding of the verb definition. Please understand, however, that it's impossible to re-create the dynamic quality of the computer lesson with a printed sample.

Let's make sure you know what I mean
when I say change tense.

Press RETURN to go on.

Tense means time, so when you change the
tense of a sentence, you change its
time.

Press RETURN to go on.

Here's an example.

  I go to this college.

What tense is this sentence in, present
or past or future?

  >it's in the present tense.

Good.

PRESENT. I go to this college.

Press RETURN to go on.

Now let's see the same sentence when I
change the tense.

PRESENT I go to this college.
        I went to this college.

What tense is this new sentence in,
present or past or future?

```
   >present

No.

The first sentence was in the present
tense. This one is in the past tense.

PRESENT  I go to this college.
PAST     I went to this college.

When I changed the tense, I changed one
word in the sentence. What word did I
change?

   >you changed went.

I mean a word in the first sentence. Try
again.

   >go

Good.

PRESENT  I go to this college.
PAST     I went to this college.

We know that go is the verb, because it
changed when we changed the tense.

Press RETURN to go on.

Now let me show you the future tense of
the same sentence.

PRESENT  I go to this college.
PAST     I went to this college.
FUTURE   I will go to this college.
```

```
Notice that the verb changed again.

Press RETURN to go on.

We can tell which words are verbs,
because they change when the tense
changes.
```

Lesson 3 helps students identify the subjects of sentences and makes sure they can identify the number (singular or plural) of those subjects. Students can do this work only after having completed Lesson 2 and must do it before they can begin to work on making verbs agree with their subjects. The next sample shows the feedback given to a student who is apparently unable to tell whether the subject of a sentence is singular or plural.

```
Now consider this sentence:

   Her brother owns four cars.

Look carefully at the subject. Is it
singular or plural?

   >pluarl

Please check your spelling and try
again.

   >plural

No. Let's review. What word is the
subject?

   >cars
```

No. You need to start with the verb.
What's the verb in this sentence?

>cars

No. Let's review. Type in here how to
identify a verb:

>it changes when you change tense.

OK. So let's rewrite this sentence in a
different tense to find the verb.
In the past tense, the sentence will
begin like this:

In 1970 her brother...

Press RETURN to go on.

Now you rewrite it in the past tense.

In 1970, her brother owned four cars

Remember, sentences end with periods.
Try again.

In 1970, her brother owned four cars.

OK. Now you know what the verb is since
you were able to change it. So what is
the verb in this sentence?

>it's owns

Now WHO is owning them?

>the brother

```
Good. So brother is the subject. Now, is
brother singular or plural?

  >singular

Good. We know it's singular because it
has no ending. Look at the same sentence
with a plural subject:

  Her brother owns four cars.
  Her brothers own four cars.
```

Only in Lesson 4 are students ready to begin working on actually making verbs agree with their subjects. They learn the concept of verb agreement and memorize the rule for making verbs agree with plural subjects. They then practice using verbs with plural noun and pronoun subjects. Finally, they rewrite a series of sentences, using plural subjects that require them to change the forms of the original verbs. The following is an example of a student working on such a sentence.

```
Now let's practice using verbs with
plural subjects or I or you.

I'll give you a sentence and then you
rewrite it with a new subject. Rewrite
this sentence:

  WANT  Edmund wants a new car.

Begin with this subject: we both

  >we both wants a new car

Remember, sentences begin with capital
letters. Try again.

  >We both wants a new car.

Remember the rule: if the subject is
```

```
plural or I or you, add no ending to the
verb. Try again.

  >We both want a new car,

Good.
```

In Lesson 5 students begin learning how to make verbs agree with singular subjects. They both see the ending on the screen and hear the sound it makes. The next sample illustrates this lesson.

```
Consider this sentence:

  COOK  My husband often ------ dinner.

Before we can fill in the verb, we need
to know the subject. So what's the
subject here?

  >the subject is husband

Is the subject singular or plural?

  >it's singluar

I don't understand your answer. Try
again.

  >it's singular

OK. Since the subject is singular, we'll
need to add an S ending to cook:

  cooks

Now listen to the sound of the ending
while I say the word:

  COOKS
```

```
The S ending shows that cooks agrees
with the singular subject husband:

COOK  My husband often cooks dinner.
```

Later in the lesson, students create verb forms, at first in isolation. As quickly as possible, though, they start using verbs in sentences with singular subjects, again by rewriting sentences. This kind of practice with forms in the context of sentences helps students to transfer what they learn in exercises to their own freely created sentences.

In Lesson 6 students work on three particularly difficult verb agreement contexts. The final program sample shows a sequence with *-es* endings. The >? prompt shows that the user wants help. The student first receives a reminder of what the principle is and then advice about what to do in this case. Again students are able to see, to write, and to hear the endings.

```
Rewrite this sentence:

  Chicken eggs hatch after 21 days.

Begin with this subject: a chicken egg

  >?

You need to rewrite this sentence with a
new subject. Decide whether the new
subject is singular or plural; then use
the appropriate form of the verb.

  >A chicken egg hatches

That's not enough words. Try again.

  >A chicken egg hatches after 21 days.

Good.
```

Further on in this lesson students work on verbs with difficult phonetic endings and on verbs where spelling changes are required. I hope eventually to be able to provide work on verbs in sentences where interrupting words (prepositional phrases or dependent clauses) occur between the subject and the verb, a pattern that often causes students to make mistakes in identifying the subject.

Future Directions

Development is under way on other modules, including a set of lessons on sentence structure. When complete, the full set of lessons should provide comprehensive instruction on the most serious grammatical problems experienced by basic writing students.

A Title III grant recently awarded to York's Educational Technology Department will allow the full-scale development of microcomputer labs in several departments of the college. As far as writing is concerned, the existing CAI program will be supplemented by microcomputer-based word processing and, possibly, heuristic programs. In addition, the program will be expanded so that there will be sufficient machinery to permit an entire class to work at one time. This will create new options for student use of computers. We will thus have at York College an integrated computer-based writing environment designed particularly for developmental students—an environment that should play a significant role in improving students' writing.

References

Allen, L. E., R. W. Allen, and J. Ross. 1970. The virtues of nonsimulation games. *Simulation and Games* 1: 319–26.

Bork, A. 1980. Interactive learning. In *The computer in the school: Tutor, tool, tutee,* ed. R. P. Taylor. New York: Teachers College Press.

Epes, M., C. Kirkpatrick, and M. G. Southwell. 1979. The COMP-LAB project: An experimental basic writing course. *Journal of Basic Writing* 2(2): 19–37.

Epes, M., C. Kirkpatrick, and M. G. Southwell. 1982. The autotutorial writing lab: Discovering its latent power. In *Tutoring writing,* ed. M. Harris. Glenview, Ill.: Scott, Foresman.

Janello, P. 1983. A study of the computer-related sessions at the 1983 CCCC with implications for the 1984 CCCC. Unpublished.

Kirkpatrick, C. 1981. The case for autotutorial materials. In *Improving writing skills,* ed. T. Hawkins and P. Brooks. San Francisco: Jossey-Bass.

Lahey, G. F. 1979. The effect of instructional presentation sequence on student performance in computer-based instruction. San Diego: Navy Personnel Research and Development Center. ERIC Document Reproduction Service No. ED 175 453.

Malone, T. W. 1980. What makes things fun to learn? A study of intrinsically motivating computer games. Report CIS-7. Palo Alto: Xerox Research Center.

Margarell, J. 1983. How faculty members use microcomputers. *The Chronicle of Higher Education,* 30 March, 10.

Piaget, J. 1954. *The construction of reality in the child.* New York: Basic Books.

Southwell, M. G. 1982a. Using computer-assisted instruction for developmental writing. *AEDS Journal* 15: 80–91.

Southwell, M. G. 1982b. Computers and developmental writing at York College/ CUNY. *The Computing Teacher,* Nov., 34–35.

Southwell, M. G. 1983. Computer-assisted instruction in composition at York College/CUNY: Grammar for basic writing students. *The Writing Instructor* 2: 165–73.

Winterowd, W. R. 1980. Developing a composition program. In *Reinventing the rhetorical tradition,* ed. A. Freedman and T. Pringle. Conway, Ark.: L&S Books.

System Requirements

The COMP-LAB Writing Modules have been programmed for Atari 400 or 800 computers with 32K RAM, a BASIC cartridge, one disk drive, and a color monitor. Earphones are recommended for use in a crowded lab.

The modules are currently being translated for use on Apple and IBM microcomputers.

Program Availability

The modules are being field tested and should be commercially available in 1984.

I wish to acknowledge the assistance of my colleague Carolyn Grinnell Kirkpatrick in preparing this chapter. Examples of CAI lessons are taken from THE COMP-LAB Writing Modules © 1983 COMP-LAB Associates and are used with permission.

III Word Processing
Research and Applications

The three chapters of Part III discuss research being done on word processors with students of various ages. Chapter 7 describes how the University of Minnesota English Department began using word processors. The authors also review research on word processors. In Chapter 8 Stephen Marcus describes both the effect of word processors on how people write and some techniques that can be used in the classroom with word processors. In the final chapter of Part III, Colette Daiute discusses how the use of word processors may affect the writing and revising of children.

7 Integrating Computers into a Writing Curriculum; or, Buying, Begging, and Building

Lillian S. Bridwell
Donald Ross
University of Minnesota

When we first began our computer project, we had what we thought was a research- and theory-based curriculum for both freshman and upper division writing courses—and we wanted to keep it that way, despite the new hardware and software that tempted us to play video games with our courses. But our students were demanding that we become "computer literate," so, with a knowledge of mainframe computers and statistical and stylistic computing in our repertoires, we set out to discover what there was available to a writing program that wanted to survive into the twenty-first century. We found very little that satisfied us in our year-long search for appropriate software (see Bridwell, Nancarrow, and Ross [1984] and Nancarrow, Ross, and Bridwell [1982] for a review and the extensive bibliography that resulted from that search).

We ran into much work of the drill and practice variety (see also Schwartz [1982] and Wresch [1982] for critiques of that kind of programming), but this hardly seemed appropriate for our advanced undergraduates in upper division writing courses, the pool for our first plunge. With more diving, we found some impressive work "under development" at a variety of institutions, both large and small (well represented by the contributors to this collection). We found several problems as we sought to pull together this work, however, problems we know others have also faced:

1. The programs were sometimes narrow in scope; for example, Burns's (1979, 1981) fine invention programs are really only one kind of invention exercise for writers, hardly enough for a comprehensive curriculum.

2. The more fully developed programs we found (e.g., Writer's Workbench) put heavy emphasis on only one aspect of writing—editing. While we, too, emphasize editing, we did not want to

privilege it over problem solving, invention, audience analysis, knowledge of text structures in different disciplines, and many other goals of our curriculum.

3. Those programs which were comprehensive in scope (e.g., the UCLA Word Processing Project) were either not yet available or the parts which we could use ran on hardware we didn't own at the time.

4. Often programs, no matter how good they were, did not allow our instructors, an amalgam of very independent thinkers, the kind of flexibility they had always been accustomed to—the ability to pick and choose among instructional materials and textbooks—and the freedom to tailor a collection of materials for their individual courses and students' needs.

5. Word processing, which we thought should be at the core of our "learn to write by writing philosophy," had not been studied for effects on composing processes.

At that point, we realized that we needed to study more carefully the appropriate goals for computers in a comprehensive writing program (not just what they *can* do, but what they *should* do), the effects of computer composing on writers, and the best purchases to make for a computer-composing environment. We obtained funding from The Fund for the Improvement of Postsecondary Education for a three-year project which would allow us to study all these areas and to develop software to meet the needs of upper division college writers, needs we felt we could address.

The Place of the Computer in the Writing Curriculum

We chose to focus our computer project on the upper division (junior and senior level) courses for both pedagogical and social reasons. Our upper division students have generally stronger motivation to learn to write and a more definite sense of the place writing will have in their lives after they graduate than do our freshmen—perhaps a cause-effect relationship. We also assumed that juniors and seniors would appreciate the potential value of computer and word processor training and experience, both for their school work and for the office or work place they hoped to move into. Another advantage from our point of view was that our upper division curriculum includes courses serving clusters of disciplines, from the arts, literature, and social sciences to preprofessional courses for engineering and business. These clusters made it possible for us to design task-specific computer aids for writers, as well as generic writing software.

While we have long endorsed the general idea that our courses need to be attentive to theories that see writing as a complex, recursive process, one of our starting points was to see how these powerful ideas manifested themselves in the classroom. Our staff of over 100 intelligent, imaginative graduate assistants naturally includes people with a wide range from orthodoxy to rebellion, and we have stressed the need to make their courses their own. While we give guidance and support, we do not try to control what happens. One hope is that the teachers will translate our attitude into a rich sense of the diversity of their students' abilities and needs. It seemed, then, that any computer-aided instruction at this level had to be selected by the individual teacher, or it had to be relatively self-contained so that students could find their own ways to it. Furthermore, we needed to provide as wide ranging a body of materials as possible, since we see writing on nearly every topic and in nearly every form now current in American society.

Before we describe the current status of our project, it is important to review some of the psychological and social effects of introducing computers into a culture, or a subculture such as a writing program. First, computers require that problems be stated in rather precise terms and that, by and large, they be broken down into relatively small pieces ("modules" or "subroutines"). This approach runs counter to many concerns of writers, especially as they write for discovery or to handle multiple, abstract problems. So we were determined to give the writers much freedom simply to think and write and keep our computing systems out of their way.

Second, a computer is an intimate medium that stresses user control. This concept is valid for a very large computer run from a terminal, but is visually obvious when everything one needs rests on a desk. It is important, then, for software to maximize the student's sense of control. We have very little need for deterministic exercises where everything from the exact response to the response time is dictated by the computer program. Open-ended exercises may guide a student through an important problem-solving heuristic, for example, but the important point here is that the student should see the computer as a tool, not a super-efficient authority.

Finally, a computer can remember lots of material which can be made available to the writer when he or she wants it, when the teacher thinks the writer needs it, or to anyone the writer chooses to share it with. Through this medium the teacher can communicate directly and even personally with the student and vice versa. The student can read what the teacher has written, and the student can store her or his own writing, from rough notes through polished, final drafts. Of course, we haven't realized the full potential of the technology. Full and instantaneous communication demands portable, compatible computers at home and in everyone's office. Even though we cannot use all the capabilities we know the computer has, due mainly to economic constraints, we can plan for them. Thus, our project had to be pragmatic for the present but adaptable to rapid change.

The First Step: Word Processing

The simplest, yet most effective leap into the computer age for writers is to use a computer for word processing. We have done this the easy way— with a microcomputer and a commercial program having a total price of about $3,000 per work station. We have utility (draft quality) printers; one printer per three computers keeps the printers busy but holds down the waiting. We allow students an average of two hours a week for computer composing, but we are increasingly encountering students who get "hooked" and want to do *all* of their writing at one of our computers.

To prepare for the first step, we did two things: (1) we studied the effects of computer composing on both experienced writers and student writers, and (2) we designed ways to introduce students to word processing quickly and efficiently.

Studies of Computer Composing Processes

Our studies of experienced writers and student writers, along with the research of others, have shown us that writers at all levels approach composing in different ways and that these different styles affect how they accommodate computer composing. We have seen a range of ways writers adjust, from those who adamantly retained their paper composing rituals and use the computer only for preparing final drafts to those who are at home with on-screen note taking, composing, revising, and editing.

A factor contributing to this range seems to be the way writers plan. If a writer uses many visual cues—diagrams, "trees," spatial indicators—she or he may have difficulty making a computer lacking sophisticated graphics capabilities work as effectively as a legal pad. Furthermore, if the writer composes many chunks of text and then determines their connections as he or she "discovers" the text's structure, the writer may prefer paper for the discovery process, simply because the size of the display screen makes it difficult to see many things simultaneously or in juxtaposition. The person who works out a global plan initially and then "executes" a written text from it makes the fastest adjustment, at least among the writers we have studied. We place no value judgments on these styles, but feel we need to develop tools for all kinds of writers. Of course, these styles are also affected by the writing task and context. We must continue to study composing processes so that we can guide both teachers and students as they search for appropriate tools.

Student Reactions to Computer Composing

The results of the first year's work with students and word processors has been mixed, but each successive quarter brings more positive results. We made a major mistake when we began. We passed out 100 floppy disks to all students who expressed an interest in doing their work on computers. We didn't realize that nearly all of them would voluntarily show up and become frustrated trying to find time on our machines. The next quarter, we limited access to four sections and developed training materials to introduce students to the programs. During the final quarter of the year, we again limited access and had four trained teachers who worked with a project assistant to introduce students to word processing, integrating this skill closely with the actual assignments in the course. This mix has been most successful, as results of student surveys demonstrate.

Out of 48 students who responded to our surveys during the third quarter (approximately 75 percent of those involved), 83 percent reported that they were able to use the computers regularly and for most of their assignments. Sixty-three percent of them described using the computer for writing as "a great advantage," 35 percent called it "a useful tool," and only one student saw it as a disadvantage. When asked whether it was useful for writing for their course, 65 percent saw it as "very useful," 33 percent as "somewhat useful," and, again, one saw it as "not very useful." A large majority, 80 percent, thought that using the computer improved their writing. None of the students thought it made their writing worse. The chief complaint was "not enough access time," a problem complicated by the fact that 48 percent of the students were composing on the screen "from start to finish" by the end of the quarter. Clearly, our students see the power of the computer to help them compose and to produce polished texts.

Training for Computer Composing

To introduce students to word processing, we designed written materials and on-screen exercises to explain the basic operations: deleting and inserting text, moving blocks, cursor movement, scrolling, etc. We found we had to rewrite the commercial descriptions of how the word processor works, especially for students who had never used one before. We produced several varieties, all of which we will continue revising until they are maximally effective. The problem seems to be confusion between learning about word processing and learning about writing. We want to focus on the latter, since we are, after all, in the writing business. Our next step in the process of integrating computer technology into our curriculum will be to have *separate* workshops for those who wish concentrated hands-on word processor training early in the quarter. In this way, we hope to avoid the "double bind" many students felt early in the course.

Our methods for introducing word processing have varied depending on which of us wrote them, indicating that we ourselves have had different learning styles as we conquered electronic writing. One of us provides handouts on everything from computer operating systems to formatting commands. Students read these before they approach the computer for the first time. Another of us draws visual diagrams and tacks them up on the walls of the lab. Students look up at the papered walls for help when they encounter a problem. Another staff member believes the only way to learn is to rely solely on the word processing package's on-screen menus and thus avoids the paper clutter altogether. Finally, we have had brave souls who actually read the commercial materials, as well as "how-to" word processing books; we will continue to make these available to students in the lab, especially for those who get interested in activities such as sophisticated formatting (e.g., proportional spacing, footnotes, headers and footers) and high-speed laser printing via mainframe computers. We've found that when we ask students what helped them most, each method has its advocates and critics; we've drawn the obvious conclusion that we should have a variety of aids available.

Beyond Word Processing

Besides helping a writer produce texts, a computer program can do at least three other things: provide information, produce feedback on texts the writer has typed in, and prompt the writer to do things in steps arranged in a linear sequence or in complicated branching and looping patterns.

Access to Information

A computer can present someone with something to read on the screen, thus becoming a communications device. Because the screen is part of a TV set, it can potentially present something other than a text—a work of art, a line drawing, video images from a cassette or disc—and it can present a spoken message or other audio material, music perhaps. Certainly for the next few years, we will focus on texts, but as libraries move toward electronic storage, we hope to be able to allow students to do much of their initial information gathering on the screen. Within the decade, they should have the possibility of bringing almost any kind of archival information into their composing environment through communication networks.

Our capabilities in this area are limited at present. However, we have explored ways to store data bases useful for social science writing, as well as ways to allow students to alternate between on-line statistical analyses of these data and writing about their findings. Specialized fields such as law and medicine already have extensive data bases which could provide the ideal connection between our students as writers and "real" information about which they might write. In a simple application, however, our instructors have begun to compile modest textfiles themselves (something an expensive optical scanner could do for them now if costs weren't a problem). They have placed, on computer disks, a number of exercises that complement textbook assignments, as well as primary texts to which students are expected to respond. Students can thus use the computer as both textbook and tablet.

Text Analysis

A computer program can analyze what the writer types in, but only within severe limits. The easiest thing to deal with is a single letter of the alphabet typed in response to a multiple choice situation. For our composition curriculum, however, this kind of exercise is of limited use.

A program can also search for specified words or phrases which the student types in. More elaborate analyses of language, whether on syntactic or semantic levels, are quite complex, slow, and liable to error rates of 10 to 20 percent. It is not feasible to expect a computer to "read," in the sense of understanding a student's piece of writing. It can, however, count things, such as *to be* verbs and words per sentence. To the extent that this information gives the writer something to ponder, this kind of program may have some value.

As we proceed through the logical problems which are a part of the writing process, computer-based strategies actually become more reliable and effective. It is difficult to program a computer to intervene "automatically" when prewriting is taking place. But some corrections don't require that the text be understood at all, the most obvious example being a mistyped or misspelled word. Many other mechanical errors and some stylistic flaws can also be targets for automatic, computer-based discovery and correction. The most elaborate programs that address these problems are Bell Laboratory's Writer's Workbench (Macdonald et al. 1982) and IBM's EPISTLE (Miller et al. 1981). The former has been used extensively for the past year at Colorado State University with positive results. (See Chapter 4 for an account of the CSU experience.) As the large corporations producing these programs improve them, we will make them available as an editing option.

In the meantime, we have discovered several adequate and easy-to-use programs for microcomputers, among them spelling checkers, an on-line thesaurus, and a grammar checker much like the Writer's Workbench STYLE and DICTION programs. Our inclination is to continue to watch for better programs from commercial sources, since we expect that automatic corrections will continue to appeal to the business world.

Another alternative in text analysis is teaming the instructor with the computer by storing and retrieving stock comments which that instructor often makes in response to students' essays. William Marling of Case Western Reserve University has designed a program of this sort, and we have negotiated (the "begging" part of our title) with him to let us try it out. No doubt, we will want to build in some of our own commentary, as well as the option to compose unique comments on the screen as we read through the text. Marling's idea, using dedicated keys to mark the text and then in another mode using the same keys so that the student can call up explanations of the commentary, makes the obvious connection between the human reader and the computer.

One immediate problem with the teacher-computer commentary system is a familiar one: access time. Most of our teachers don't have computers where they read papers (at home, for example), and it takes time to do the file management required to read student papers, at least in the floppy disk medium. Marling reports that computer grading takes him longer, but he thinks it is worth the investment. Similar problems will emerge when we try to set up "electronic conference groups." The technology makes it possible to produce a copy of a student's text with collated marginal comments from a number of peer readers, for example. This draft can then stimulate the writer to incorporate or reject feedback from many sources. However, students need much screen time to read and react to each other's papers, and until they have more access to the computers, we will have to use these techniques experimentally.

Intervening in the Writing Process

A computer can also prompt a writer to respond, using either linear sequences or recursive branches or loops. The latter can be driven either by the responses themselves or by the writer who selects options at various points. These programs, often called computer-assisted instruction, are the most demanding part of designing a computer writing curriculum because they require anticipating the writer's needs at all points. Most of the initial work in this area has been either quite general, as in the case of Burns's invention programs (1979), described in Chapter 1, or tied to a specific assignment, such as Schwartz's literature analysis program (1982), described in Chapter 3—largely because it is so difficult to design programs suitable to a variety of contexts. In our project, we will use such programs where they are effective, but we are also constantly searching for ways to put more control into the hands of the writer. We can speculate about the "computing composer," the writer who knows enough programming to write programs that solve her or his unique writing problems. (We do, by the way, know some engineers who are already "computing composers," writing their own software to solve the sticky problems of including mathematical formulae in their reports.) For the time being, however, the average student will not be able to tackle problems like this.

Invention Exercises

One way of thinking about computer aids to invention, at least in the context of the composition class, is that they are enhancements of assignment making. If a teacher just says, "Write a paper," and gives a due date, there's not much a computer program can do beyond some standard pattern like "Limit your topic." Once the students settle on something, however, programs like Burns's that guide them through Aristotle's topoi, Burke's pentad, or Pike's tagmemic analysis can invite them to explore the topic. The student sees a series of questions and responds with a line or so. A typical question will accommodate the topic, "What has been the historical attitude toward *welfare*?" Burns claims that the approach increases student interest and produces more formal first drafts.

During our review of our upper division courses, we paid special attention to what teachers ask of their students, both in terms of the topics they suggest and the degree to which they try to specify the rhetorical and pragmatic context. The programs we are designing invite students to engage in fairly extensive audience analysis through several strategies, ranging from a formal audience profile (almost like a questionnaire or a fictional curriculum vitae) through other, freer ways that people try to conceptualize the "other mind" who might read the paper. We use the same range of approaches to have the student define the persona he or she will try to project in an essay and, of course, invite efforts to explain and narrow the gap that exists between the implied audience and implied narrator. A third kind of invention aid invites students to explore their relationship to the knowledge they are acquiring and expressing about their topic, a "writing to learn" approach.

Some of our courses, especially engineering and business writing, properly include assignments that demand adherence to traditional genres and formats. The reader of a research report expects information to be in a set sequence and expects certain content and even a well-defined linguistic style in each section. We will emulate the advice about such formats found in better textbooks for these courses. We expect to use questions that invite the student to answer at whatever length seems appropriate. The answers can then be merged, linked, and printed. In addition, we will provide optional, on-screen commentary on differing rhetorical and stylistic expectations. The whole area should provide us with a difficult challenge: format-driven papers are often dull or trivial, since some students think that matching the format is a substitute for critical thinking. (We do not want to foster more five-paragraph themes by declaring a thesis should look like "All Gaul is divided into three parts" for every essay.) On the other hand, when an assignment is only stated as "Discuss . . ." or "Explain . . .," the student's failure to discover a meaningful structure often leads to thoughts spread in near random order. Such papers show little sensitivity to any audience, living or dead.

While assignments in many areas of the humanities, including writing about literature, do not have well-defined formats, our initial survey shows some consistent patterns of thought that students are expected to follow as they generate material on a play or a painting. As we continue to seek possible invention (or problem-solving) aids, we are exploring such topics as "methods of proof" in various disciplines.

Drafting and Revising

Once students have used whatever invention aids they need to get started, they may be able simply to execute their plan. If this is the case, then the best thing we could do for them would be to clear the screen, provide a fast and efficient word processing program, and get out of the way. Occasionally, students may need to look at their outlines, if they made one, or to read some information on the screen, so they need a quick way in and out of different computer-stored documents. At present, we do not have a quick way to access files generated by different systems or through communication networks. Until we can provide this, the writer is better off with paper and pencil, notes from the library, paper-clipped book pages, and photocopied passages next to the keyboard.

Students may, however, need ongoing help with problem solving and invention. Software aids like split screens can allow a writer to generate notes on troublesome ideas while producing parts of the text that come easily. Other hardware gadgets like light pens and graphics screens could also help with trees, Venn diagrams, circles and crosses, and any other visual aids students might use to solve writing problems. If they change their minds drastically and need to rearrange the text, they need an efficient way to move big blocks around. Existing computer technology makes all of these things possible, but we have not found a single package that meets all the needs of the range of student writers we teach, nor do we expect to find one. UCLA's WANDAH, under development by Ruth Von Blum and Michael Cohen and described in Chapter 11, comes closest to combining word processing with composing, and we are currently field testing it as it is being developed.

The split screen mode on many word processing packages also makes possible interactive prompts to foster effective revision—suggestions can appear on the screen automatically or when writers ask for "revision help" and further specify what kind they need. We have already mentioned the electronic conference group and teacher commentary (the latter can be called up during drafting and revising). Also, writers can provide their own catalysts by making ongoing notes and comments on a separate section of their screen. An alternative is a symbol system to place notes and comments embedded in a text (e.g., "Come back to this point later when I know what I'm doing."); a "strip" program can automatically delete them before the draft is printed.

Integrating It All with Students and Teachers

The theme of our discussion has been tailoring computer programs to the interests and needs of individual students, teachers, courses, and occasions. Ours is a large program—thousands of students a year—and we can't afford the luxury of developing a few elegant programs for only a few sections. That is, we can't if we bear in mind a significant computer-age issue: equal opportunity. We are very much concerned that we not favor our engineering or computer science majors over our liberal arts students. Nor do we want to design programs that privilege the computer editor over the computer composer. Nor do we want to increase the gap between students who have computers at home and those who rely on us for access. These are all tremendous problems for a public institution that can't afford to provide a computer for everyone and can't require one of entering students.

One of our solutions is a general-purpose program that will set up a screen sequence of information, questionnaires, and choices. Teachers will then be able to write their own material without knowing how to program, or they will be able to change someone else's sequences. In the jargon of the field, we have begun to design an authoring system and have settled on its preliminary specifications. Such a system will let us make rapid progress in developing materials for many of our courses, and it will let us tap the resources of excellent writing teachers who have no need (and no desire) to spend their precious hours tinkering with programming languages.

We will apply our administrative resources to make the environment as responsive to individual demands as possible, while at the same time tackling the general programming needs that cannot be met by the authoring system. We are, for example, investigating ways of making textfiles produced with a variety of computers and software packages compatible with each other so that students and teachers have more resources at their typing fingertips. And finally, we will continue to study the effects of computers on the developing writing abilities of our students. This calls for an objective and sometimes critical stance toward the computer in the writer's world. We strongly hope that such efforts will make it easier for students and teachers to build on the computer's remarkable possibilities.

References

Bridwell, L., P. R. Nancarrow, and D. Ross. 1984. The writing process and the writing machine: Current research on word processors relevant to the teaching of composition. In *New directions in composition research,* ed. R. Beach and L. Bridwell, 381–98. New York: Guilford Press.

Burns, H. 1979. Stimulating invention in English composition through computer-assisted instruction. Ph.D. dissertation, University of Texas, Austin.

———. 1981. Pandora's chip: Concerns about quality CAI. *Pipeline,* Fall, 15–16, 49.

Macdonald, N. H., L. T. Frase, P. Gingrich, and S. A. Keenan. 1982. The Writer's Workbench: Computer aids for text analysis. *IEEE Transactions on Communication* 30: 105–10.

Miller, L. A., G. E. Heidorn, and K. Jensen. 1981. Text-critiquing with the EPISTLE system: An author's aid to better syntax. *Proceedings of the National Computer Conference,* Anaheim, Calif.

Nancarrow, P. R., D. Ross, and L. Bridwell. 1982. Word processors and the writing process: An annotated bibliography. University of Minnesota, Department of English. Mimeo.

Schwartz, H. 1982. Monsters and mentors: Computer applications for humanistic education. *College English* 44 (Feb.): 141–52.

Wresch, W. 1982. Computers in English class: Finally beyond grammar and spelling drills. *College English* 44 (Sept.): 483–90.

Program Availability

The authors' use of the programs listed here is in a constant state of flux. As we continue to review the available software, we will subtract, add to, or replace those programs we now use. There are no hard and fast rules about what we will select. Current software now in use in the University of Minnesota's Computer Lab for the Program in Composition and Communication are as follows:

Word Processing Packages

WANDAH, UCLA (commercially forthcoming). The ultimate in a simple program for those unfamiliar with word processing.

WordStar, MicroPro International. A very popular and widely used program.

Final Word, Mark of the Unicorn. Offers technical sophistication for formatting; especially useful for technical writers and engineers.

Style and Mechanics Checking

WANDAH (appropriate sections)

Proofreader, Random House

Grammatik, Aspen Software

Problem-Solving Software for Disciplines

Abstat. For statistics and for writing in the quantitative social sciences.

Data Base Management Packages, e.g., d-Base II and Lotus 1-2-3. For writing in business and for organizing references for extended pieces of writing.

Authoring System

Access—A Comprehensive Composing Educational Software System. A set of programs under development at the University of Minnesota that allows teachers to develop their own computer-assisted materials for individual writing classes.

8 Real-Time Gadgets with Feedback: Special Effects in Computer-Assisted Writing

Stephen Marcus
University of California, Santa Barbara

The catchy phrase in the title is a characterization drawn from John D. Gould's research (1981) at IBM. He was comparing people's use of word processors with their performance in preparing hand-written documents. Noting that people spent more time than actually needed working with the computers, he suggested that this was in part because the machines were simply fun to use, like pinball machines, video games, and roulette wheels—real-time gadgets with feedback. This chapter explores the unique qualities of this new composing gadget, that is, the special attributes of the technology itself which give the writer new powers and incentives.[1]

Invisible Writing with Computers

Peter Elbow and a host of others have long advocated the practice of "freewriting" as a technique to develop fluency and as an appropriate tool in the prewriting stage of the composing process. The emphasis in freewriting is on the flow of thought rather than on attention to the details of grammar, spelling, or punctuation. Recent experiments we have been conducting (Marcus and Blau 1983) suggest that word processors can provide a special environment for freewriting. Simply by adjusting the brightness knobs on their monitors, students can eliminate immediate visual feedback yet still record their ideas. The text may eventually be examined by brightening the screen display, and as usual, it is available for editing, saving, and printing. Students commonly reported that when they wrote under ordinary circumstances, they usually would allow their minds to wander; rarely did they focus their attention undeviatingly on a single train of thought for more than one or two sentences. In addition, students noted that their usual pattern in composing was to interrupt the flow of thought frequently to edit and amend the language, syntax, and mechanics of their text. Invisible writing experiments suggested to them

120

that their usual pauses obstruct their fluency and, more importantly, dilute their concentration. Under the conditions of the experiment, they could neither edit nor rewrite, nor could they allow their attention to stray from the line of thought they were developing.

Invisible writing with computers discouraged the kind of "local editing" that is particularly common with word processors and that is counterproductive at certain stages of the composing process. It encouraged a quality of attention to the topic at hand which is sometimes lacking in usual freewriting activities. Not everyone, of course, found it a congenial procedure, even after practice. Still, for many students, invisible writing helped them see how premature editing interfered with their writing, and it brought into sharp relief their own tendencies and compulsions in this regard. In the words of one student, "Invisible writing helped me understand that writing really begins with prewriting."

The Moving Cursor Having Writ . . . .

. . . can erase or copy all of it.[2] The cursor, that blinking pulse of the machine, can do much more, of course. A significant event in our computer literacy workshops for English and language arts teachers is participants' first experience with their power over the cursor. Their ability to move "physically" through words without altering them demonstrates to teachers the fluidity of videotext (the term is discussed at more length below). Like invisible writing, working with the cursor develops an awareness of the actual relationship between what writers see on the screen and what they will eventually get. It helps them acquire the perspective that allows a writer, or teacher of writing, to fully exploit the medium.

One of the earliest to adapt the technology to writing instruction was James Joyce, then at the University of California, Berkeley. Joyce's students were using a word processing system that automatically filled out the lines when the text was printed. Lines displayed on the screen could be of any length; when the printed copy was produced, space on each line was filled with text and justified. Joyce recommended that students enter their text a phrase to a line. Aside from making later editing easier, this method allowed students to notice more easily whether their phrases tended to be too long or short, helped the writers to focus on discrete semantic units, and encouraged them to develop syntactical maturity through sentence combining activities. Joyce (1981) also suggested that in some cases of writer's block, the simple act of scrolling text up the screen "literally got things moving again. This had worked successfully when all that was being formatted was the title, name of the author, and the author's address."

For many students, seeing words dance around a screen—with procedures and special function keys like search-and-replace, move-text, delete, retype—generates quite a different sense of the risk involved in committing themselves to writing. They no longer feel their words to be "carved in stone" (often the stone of writer's block). Instead, their words have the quality of light. Their sentences slide back and forth, ripple down the screen, become highlighted, disappear, and reappear. This versatility can be used for specific exercises.

One of the practice files we have developed is based on the "first line/last line" idea made popular with our project by Dick Dodge of the UCLA Writing Project. When students load the SCREEN SCENES file into their word processor, they see two apparently unrelated sentences, for example:

```
He checked his schedule to see what he
planned to ruin today. They left him
wondering whether the door would close
in time.
```

The directions are to move the cursor between the sentences and to type in a story that connects them. As the writers do, they see the second (i.e., final) sentence creep to the right, snaking down the screen as they continue typing. If they can develop a coherent sequence of events before the concluding sentence disappears off the bottom of the screen, all the better. It is not a necessary objective, but it proves to be an interesting and challenging one. Exercises like this provide opportunities for practicing cursor control and for increasing coherence, unity, etc. They also immerse the student in the medium's more subtle message: their words are not fixed and rigid. Expression has shape and movement, literally and figuratively.

Making the Implicit Explicit

While activities like freewriting attempt to turn the inner voice off in the service of fluency, some researchers are attempting to turn it up in order to study and perhaps to train it. This is the composing-out-loud technique used by Janet Emig (1971), Sondra Perl (1980), and others. There are intriguing relationships between the transcripts of such sessions and the records generated by computer-assisted prewriting tutorials. Such tutorials include Helen Schwartz's SEEN program (1982) for exploring topics in literature; Hugh Burns's three heuristic programs (1980) based on Aristotle's topoi, Burke's pentad, and the Young, Becker, and Pike tagmemic matrix; and William Wresch's Writer's Helper (1982a, 1982b), which helps students develop the substance of different kinds of essays but does the formatting and paragraph construction by itself. (See Chapters 3, 1, and 10 for a detailed look at these programs.) Additionally, Andee Rubin (1980) and her colleagues have developed computer-assisted activities to help children write stories, while our work (Marcus 1982a, 1982b) at Santa Barbara has included courseware for helping students (fourth grade through graduate school) study and write poetry.

While the composing-out-loud research has attempted to elicit the writer's own inner dialogue, computer-assisted tutorials such as the ones cited above, although not necessarily designed with this in mind, function to create a sort of ideal inner dialogue (or the kind of productive office hour that teachers dream about). The hope, of course, is that students will eventually internalize the procedures and not merely rely on the machines for guidance. In these tutorials, the computer (not a word processor in the usual sense of the phrase) provides the effective problem-solving strategies and positive feedback so noticeably absent in many of the research transcripts, which are instead filled with irrelevant or counterproductive inner dialogue and self-generated negative feedback. By virtue of using such computer-assisted tutorials, students are provided with an immediate transcript, a kind of composing-out-loud protocol to serve as record and resource for future drafts.

Along with procedures for peer editing, we have been experimenting with computer-assisted collegial prewriting, again by utilizing the special attributes of the medium.[3] We have tried combining a modified version of invisible writing with the "writing consultant" approach implicit in the tutorials discussed above. Our word processing systems run on microcomputers that have video monitors connected by wire to the keyboard/computer. We simply have the students sitting next to each other exchange monitors, so that Student A's monitor, still connected to Student A's computer, rests atop Student B's computer. Student B's monitor rests on Student A's computer. The monitors are angled slightly to discourage peeking. As Student A begins prewriting on a topic, the text appears in front of Student B. If Student A loses her train of thought, she types "???" whereupon Student B types a response such as "You were talking about. . . ." If Student A runs out of ideas, she types "XXX." Student B may then suggest a new line of thought, or he might develop an additional perspective on A's current thought. Student A may use or reject the suggestion. When the students print their respective files, Student A has the text, and Student B has the record of assistance. The two files together constitute a record of collaboration for further study and discussion and for use in Student A's next draft.

This kind of activity utilizes the advantages of freewriting and invisible writing and adds to them the benefits of training students to be careful readers, paraphrasers, and writing consultants. Students are writing for an audience that actually responds to the meaning of their text—something that the computer programs for tutorials do not do (they are essentially GI-GO systems: garbage in, garbage out). While this application of invisible writing is in certain ways not as productive as the tutorials, the procedure does have benefits not available with the programs, not the least of which is that it maintains in a very definite way the social dimension of the composing process and the sense of audience. It also provides a temporary antidote to the isolation some people feel when working with computers.

Pruning the Trees, Shaping the Forest

Several quite powerful revision and editing programs exist that will read a student's paper and provide information on sentence type, paragraph structure, sexist language, wordiness and use of clichés, readability, use of passive voice and nominalization, or sentence-length variablity. Teachers overburdened with 500-word themes to grade may react with some ambivalence to the knowledge that a computer can process a paper in less time than it takes to read this sentence. IBM's EPISTLE, Westinghouse's Writing Aids System, Bell Laboratories' Writer's Workbench, the U.S. Navy's Computer Readability Editing System, and HOMER at UCLA are all examples of programs designed to improve writing by examining text, providing feedback on surface structure, and suggesting improvements. Interesting research is under way by, among others, Kiefer and Smith at Colorado State University, who are studying the transference in college students from computer-aided to self-initiated editing habits (see Chapter 4); by Bill King at the University of California, Davis, who has examined the high correlation between the scores assigned to papers by readers and by a computer's text analysis; and by Colette Daiute at Harvard University, who has studied changes in the revising procedures of children who are using word processing programs with writing-related prompts (see Chapter 9).

Text analysis programs like the ones mentioned above are machine-specific, and only a few, like HOMER, are available for microcomputers. In addition, while some are very fast, others are quite slow (by computing standards). Still, the speed with which a word processor can accomplish even a global search-and-replace (SAR) instills a significant number of people with a new sense of power when it comes to editing and revising their text.

One of our demonstration/practice files, SHERLOCK, consists of a passage from a Sherlock Holmes story in which certain vowels have been replaced by symbols (there is an additional substitution just to make things interesting). This results in a rather long series of lines which seem at first glance to be total "garbage" as they scroll up the screen. For example: 7nxgl!nc7ngx?v$rxmyxn?t$sx?fxth$s$v-

The task is to decode the file by practicing global SAR procedures, i.e., having the computer search for every occurrence of a given symbol and replace it with the indicated vowel. Since this activity often occurs in workshop settings with no written instructions for instituting an SAR, the participants are led through one or two substitutions to teach them the key-press procedures. When asked to count the number of seconds required for the first substitution actually to take place, there is predictable amazement when they see it completed before anyone reaches "One." It's happened before they've quite understood that it could have happened.

A more practical revision example is to have the workshop participants load the THREE TO ONE file which consists of a narrative passage written in third-person singular. The task is to transform it to first-person singular using only four SAR procedures. Although this activity, along with ones such as SHERLOCK, is designed to demonstrate and practice specific key-press sequences and editing functions, the major initial effect is to immerse the novice in an environment in which the computer does tricks with words, serving to illustrate Arthur C. Clarke's adage that "any sufficiently advanced technology is indistinguishable from magic." Gould (1981) has suggested that it is the attraction to this "magic show" that keeps even writers experienced with word processors fiddling with their texts. Others, such as Ruth Von Blum at UCLA, have noted that local editing of words and sentences can interfere with ongoing development of text (partly for this reason, she has included invisible writing in her

WANDAH program). Perhaps this narrow focus inhibits the broader perspective needed to reconceptualize large units or to alter stylistic features. This broader perspective can be provided by the text analysis programs mentioned earlier, which although sometimes limited in scope, are constantly being made more sophisticated and accessible. Even without access to one of these analysis programs, it is still possible to provide this larger perspective, for example, with SAR procedures like those described above. In one case, a teacher working with sixth graders had been using a word processor with them for months but had not thought to have them work with SAR. A brief experience with SHERLOCK and THREE TO ONE was all she needed to begin her own creative applications, including transforming students' poems about plant life cycles into poems about their own life cycles.

The Muse and the Machine

The mystifying and engrossing effects of computers have not been limited to prose writing. The linking of computers, poets, and poetry has occurred in at least five regards: (1) poetry written with the aid of word processors, (2) poetry written on the subject of computers, (3) poetry redefined by virtue of new computer-based forms, (4) computer-generated poetry, and (5) poetry written with interactive software that guides the writer in the form and content of the poem. This last-named area is the focus of a Computers and Poetry Project (CPP) combining technology and imagination to provide a certain "sleight of mind."[4]

The objectives of the CPP are to provide students and teachers (grades 4–12) with novel approaches to the study and writing of poetry, to increase their computer literacy in the language arts, and to develop courseware that is consistent with California State Department of Education guidelines for language arts instruction. Some 20 teachers and approximately 500 students are using and evaluating Compupoem, a program being redesigned for specific grade levels (Marcus 1982a, 1982b).

Compupoem engages the students in all phases of the composing process: prewriting, writing, and rewriting. It prompts them for parts of speech, juggles their words into a poetic form, provides advice on choosing such things as prepositional phrases, adverbs, and nouns—and on Zen in the art of computer-assisted writing. It also allows them to see their poems instantly rewritten in different formats (including as a sentence) in order to, for example, study the relationships between the form and the impact of words.

Students using Compupoem do prewriting at an astonishing pace. Even their first drafts can display a striking level of diction and richness of image. Although many of the early drafts are more like diamonds in the rough, they still deserve and reward the reader's attention. They focus on some specific image or event, directing the reader to note its beauty, significance, or humor.

Early discussions of such computer-assisted poetry writing have suggested the particular benefits derived from using a "real-time gadget with feedback" in the composing process (Marcus 1982a, 1982b). Questions about the nature of authorship, of poetry itself, of "what parts of speech are *doing* in a sentence" (as one student put it) were given a new vitality by incorporating unfamiliar tools into the language arts arena, reaffirming the adage about developing creativity by "making the strange familiar and the familiar strange."

Some Concluding Remarks

A good deal of what has been considered here revolves around what students see (or don't see) on their screens. Print which appears on television screens may be neither print, per se, nor television. Rather, it is print-on-television: a new medium with its own characteristic messages. In a study of children and electronic text—what I choose to call "videotext"—William Paisley and Milton Chen (1982) of Stanford University's Institute for Communications Research suggest that while television "undermined the functional basis of literacy . . . the technologies (of electronic text systems) depend *more* on literacy than even print media. At the same time, it is possible that intrinsically motivating aspects of electronic text use may cause children to read more, and at an earlier age." (Italics in original.) Certainly this may be true for writing as well as reading, particularly if, as MIT's Seymour Papert has suggested, children may soon be learning to write at the same time as they are learning to speak.

It may perhaps be true that word processors designed especially for students, like the Bank Street Writer, owe their success in part to the fact that they are easy for teachers to learn. (It is of note that fifth and sixth graders can fairly easily master a relatively complex system like Apple Writer 2.0.) Nevertheless, it is the chance to play with a real-time gadget with feedback which may prove to be of primary importance in students' willingness to develop computer-assisted writing skills. This intrinsically motivating aspect of computers in general, and of videotext specifically, deserves special attention and study. Seminal work on what makes computer games fun has been done by Thomas W. Malone (1981), initially at Stanford University and currently at the Xerox Palo Alto Research

Center. His discussions of challenge, fantasy, and curiosity in connection with computer games can enrich and inform any development of computer-assisted writing instruction, from arcade-style word games and skill-building activities to more sedate and cerebral exercises like the SCREEN SCENES assignment described above.

Videotext generates interesting questions about reading from and writing for television screens. Von Blum at UCLA is one of several researchers examining how instructional text should come to appear on the screen; possibilities include a screenful at a time, in semantic units, in units changing from a word to a phrase depending on the person's reading level. And who should control the speed at which the words appear? The reader? The teacher? The computer, based on the reader's response time? If parts of speech can be color-coded, as they already can be to a certain extent, will it help some students if we "paint" a passage from Hemingway and compare it to the mosaic produced by a passage from Faulkner? This gives new meaning to the term *language arts,* and it might be a boon to the more visually oriented students in their attempts to discern an author's style. Will it help to paint successive drafts of some students' essays, so they can see in a new way how their writing may be changing?

As more people's jobs involve writing "readable TV"—computer-assisted instruction, electronic mail, teletext and viewdata systems, captioned TV—what will the effects be on reading and writing behavior? Harold Innis noted in *The Bias of Communication* that the use of a new medium of communication over a long period will to some extent determine the character of knowledge to be communicated. Individuals who already are practiced in creating videotext are finding that writing for television screens alters their sense of the structure of knowledge and of the language conventions used to express it (see, for example, Winsbury [1979]). They experience demands for a degree of visual and design awareness that they did not initially possess. Spelling, punctuation, and paragraph structure are altered to conform to the limitations (or perhaps strengths) of the medium.

All this may seem far afield from the initial considerations of how computers can be used in writing classes. Such considerations are grounded, however, in the almost galvanic "jump for joy," the actual physical response evidenced by many people when they first see their words dancing on the screen, not carved in stone but electric and fluid. Neil Postman, discussing information environments in *Teaching as a Conserving Activity,* notes that there are important consequences to changing the form of information, its quantity, speed, or direction. Teachers and students involved in computer-assisted writing instruction are helping shape a new environment even as they are being shaped by it.

Notes

1. Part of the work reported here has been done in beginning and advanced composition classes in cooperation with Mark Ferrer, director of the Program for Intensive English, and with Steve Miko, professor of English, both of whom use word processing extensively with their classes.

2. This ditty is taken from the tutorial to *Programming the Apple Computer*, published by the Apple Computer Corporation.

3. The procedure described here was originally inspired by a conversation with Terri Cook, a doctoral student in the UCSB Confluent Education Program.

4. The Computers and Poetry Project was initiated by a grant from the Apple Education Foundation. Additional support was provided by the South Coast Writing Project, the UCSB Graduate School of Education, and the Santa Barbara County Schools Office.

References

Burns, H. 1980. Stimulating invention through computer-assisted instruction. *Educational Technology* 20.

Emig, J. 1971. *The composing processes of twelfth graders.* National Council of Teachers of English Research Report no. 13. Urbana, Ill.: NCTE.

Gould, J. D. 1981. Composing letters with computer-based text editors. *Human Factors* 23 (Oct.): 593–606.

Joyce, J. 1981. UNIX aids for English composition courses. Paper read at the Western Educational Computing Conference, San Francisco, Calif.

Malone, T. W. 1981. Toward a theory of intrinsically motivating instruction. *Cognitive Science* 4.

Marcus, S. 1982a. Compupoem: A computer-assisted writing activity. *English Journal* 71 (Feb.): 96–99.

———. 1982b. The muse and the machine: A computers and poetry project. *Classroom Computer News,* Nov./Dec.

Marcus, S., and S. Blau. 1983. Not seeing is relieving: Invisible writing with computers. *Educational Technology,* April, 12–15.

Paisley, W., and M. Chen. 1982. Children and electronic text: Challenges and opportunities of the "new literacy." NIE study, Institute for Communication Research.

Perl, S. 1980. Understanding composing. *College Composition and Communication* 31 (Dec.): 363–69.

Rubin, A. 1980. Making stories, making sense. *Language Arts* 57 (March): 285–93.

Schwartz, H. 1982. A computer program for invention and audience feedback. Paper read at the Annual Conference on College Composition and Communication, San Francisco, Calif.

Winsbury, R. 1979. *The electronic bookstall.* London: International Institute of Communications.

Wresch, W. 1982a. Prewriting, writing, and editing by computer. Paper read at the Annual Conference on College Composition and Communication, San Francisco, Calif.

———. 1982b. Computers in English class: Finally beyond grammar and spelling drills. *College English* 44 (Sept.): 483–90.

9 Can the Computer Stimulate Writers' Inner Dialogues?

Colette Daiute
Harvard University

These comments by two junior high school students suggest that the computer can have varied effects on young writers:

> The computer shows me my mistakes.
> The computer helps me see what the reader won't understand.

Some students who use programs intended to stimulate composing and revising may view the computer as an authority, a power they once gave teachers. But other students learn to control their own writing processes after they have done guided composing or revising on the computer. The purpose of my Computers and Writing Project has been to identify the cognitive causes of children's writing difficulties and the role of the computer in overcoming some of these difficulties. The main focus of the project has been to determine whether computer analysis and prompting programs can stimulate children to reflect on their own writing and improve it.

A Description of the Project

The Computers and Writing Project has included several studies and development efforts that began at Teachers College, Columbia University, and have continued at the Harvard Graduate School of Education. The Spencer Foundation has funded the three-year research project "The Effects of Automatic Prompting on Young Writers." The research has been a series of classroom- and lab-based studies on the effects of using computers for writing. The Apple Education Foundation funded our efforts to develop a method for teaching children to type, an important skill for interacting with computers. As the principal investigator, I have collaborated with colleagues Robert P. Taylor, Thomas G. Bever, and myriad graduate students. One of the main settings for the research has been the classroom of Arthur Shield in an inner city public school that has eight Apple II Plus microcomputers. The other research site has been my lab, where children from private schools, public schools, and home instruction situations have come to do their writing with computers as well as with pens and pencils.

Our research goal has been to study children's abilities to revise their own writing. Revising is an interesting cognitive activity to study because it is difficult, and many writing researchers and teachers have found it to be important (e.g., Sommers 1980). Children's revising behaviors offer evidence of cognitive processes. As children revise their writing, we can see evidence of their intellectual development, such as the ability to reflect on their own thought processes, and evidence suggestive of effective writing instruction methods.

The computer seemed to be an appropriate tool for stimulating revision because word processing programs allow writers to change their texts by giving commands rather than by recopying. Young writers usually report that writing is easier on a computer because "you don't have to recopy"; "recopying hurts your hands and is boring" (Daiute 1982). Computers can also be used to present writers with comments about their texts and to teach them to touch-type.

In our study, we are exploring the value of teaching children to pose questions about their writing so they can read over their work critically rather than simply skim over it and say, "It's fine." When writers reread and rework their drafts, the creative process continues beyond the initial composing process. Although some experienced writers do most of their planning and revising in their heads, many writers shape their pieces by doing extensive revising (Sommers 1980). They use drafts as notes and idea stimulators. In these drafts they discover what they want to say, or they record information to restructure later into an order a reader can follow. Our study is devoted to finding out if such creative rethinking is possible and beneficial for young writers.

Writers and researchers have suggested that word processing programs can reduce some of the physical difficulties of revising because they eliminate the chore of recopying. But there are limitations. To compose quickly and freely, writers must know how to type. The word processing program can create problems if it has a cumbersome command system; also, the writer must know the computer keyboard to get the maximum benefit from the program. Adult writers tend to feel free to compose on word processors because changes are easy to make (e.g., McWilliams 1982). The computer can also reduce some of the cognitive burdens on writers. The interactiveness of program commands and messages heightens writers' sense of the audience (Daiute 1983). Some researchers have reported that displaying word processing commands for deleting or moving text can suggest to young writers that they revise. In addition to the basic word processing features, text analysis and prompting programs also offer writers suggestions on basic and complex composing and revising activities.

Developing Catch

The children whose comments opened this chapter were talking about a program called Catch when they referred to "the computer." We developed Catch to provide an easy-to-use word processing program and to stimulate children's revising. When the writer requests help in looking over a text he or she has composed on the computer, Catch offers 14 types of text analyses and comments. We developed the program options based on three general criteria: first, the types of changes required to make texts clear, complete, organized, and correct according to standards of written English; second, the questions about process and form that writers tend to pose to themselves; and third, the types of analyses the computer can do.

The writer using Catch presses the "Ctrl" key and the "C" key to see a list of the program options, which includes checking to make sure that the point of the piece is stated and developed and checking sentence structure, word use, and spelling. Because of the computer's limited language-analysis capacities, some of the Catch features are quite general. For example, one option presents each paragraph of the text with this comment at the bottom of the screen: "Does this paragraph have a clear focus? If yes, press y; if no, press n." If the writer presses "y," the program checks the next paragraph. If the writer presses "n," the program presents another prompt suggesting that she or he add a topic sentence, reorganize the paragraph, or develop two paragraphs.

Other Catch options offer more concrete information. For example, one feature identifies sentences that are several words longer than the average sentence in the text. Other options identify words, such as *kind of* and *stuff*, that are usually vague or unnecessary. As the words are highlighted on the screen, a prompt appears, for instance, "The highlighted words may be too vague. If so, give more specific information."

These general and specific analyses and prompts in Catch are intended to help children review and improve their writing rather than simply correct their errors. The program helps writers focus their attention and pose questions to themselves about their own writing; the decisions and rewriting are left up to the child. Sometimes, for example, a child erases the word *very* when the program identifies it. But we have also seen many children make comments like, "No, I need that word to sound strong." These children view Catch as helping *them* find the problems in their writing. They do not follow the program suggestions by rote.

Developing the Catch Word Processor

For a full year, we observed several children between 10 and 13 years of age using word processing and text editing programs popular at the time. We noted when the children had trouble and the types of explanations that helped them, and we asked them what would have made the program easier to use. We found that children learned to use all the editors, even the line-based type that requires the user to refer to the number of the line where the text is stored. Nevertheless, the children had a much easier time learning and using programs that did not depend upon mode switching, which requires extra commands to move between composing and editing. (Many word processing programs for microcomputers involve mode switching because it requires less sophisticated programming and less computer memory than programs without mode switching.)

Once we identified the list of the most important commands and an efficient training model, we developed our own program to capture the best features of all the programs. Another reason for writing our own program was to incorporate the Catch features, which were central to our study. We developed and tested our prototype word processing and Catch program on a DEC 20 mainframe computer so we could devote our initial energy to creating an editor that was easy to use without worrying about microcomputer limits such as storage space and programming language. We wrote two versions, one with single keystroke commands and one with the more typical two keystroke commands. Eight children used these programs for about 25 hours over a five-week period. We found that the children learned and used the single keystroke editor more efficiently. We noted features of the design and program messages that posed problems.

In the second year, we refined the programs to eliminate the difficult features and rewrote them to run on an Apple II Plus. We then tested the editor and Catch at three sites: a private middle school, a public middle school, and our lab. We found that the method of introducing children to the computer and the programs was important in making them comfortable with the new "pencil." We also learned that each student needs from one to two hours a week with the computer to complete assignments efficiently and to learn the system fast enough for it to make a difference in their writing. We found that knowledge of the keyboard was important in using the computer for writing. The typing program we developed and tested teaches young writers to touch-type common letter and word sequences and thus offers them a new writing tool after the first time they use it.

Testing Catch

After we rewrote the programs on the Apple and worked out the bugs, we conducted extensive pilot testing of the prototype Catch. This test yielded detailed information for further refining of the programs as well as preliminary information about the effects of automatic writing on the development of young writers' self-monitoring skills.

Eight nine- to 12-year-old subjects wrote with the Catch word processing program for 15 hours over a five-week period. The subjects wrote drafts and revisions on nine autobiographical topics. With pen and paper, they wrote pre- and post-treatment writing samples and a short story. Using the Catch word processing program, the children wrote five-part autobiographies, two short stories, and a piece on a topic they chose.

The subjects were trained to touch-type and to use the computer programs. The subjects used Catch to stimulate revising after they said that they had improved the piece as much as they possibly could without any help. We compared the subjects' writing on the computer before and after they used the Catch prompting with their writing in pen with no prompting. All writing samples were analyzed for number of words, sentence complexity, revisions, errors, composing style, and quality.

The amount and nature of change between drafts and completed texts was the main measure of self-monitoring in this study. We predicted that the more revising the subject did, the more self-monitoring he or she had done. We adapted Faigley's and Witte's (1980) revision taxonomy for our analyses. The taxonomy categorizes the types of changes made in a draft, such as substituting one word for another or adding a paragraph, and distinguishes between meaningful and superficial changes. The taxonomy also defines revisions that significantly alter the overall meaning and purpose of the text and those that do not. These are useful distinctions for a revision analysis. For example, if subjects make more changes in response to prompting, but the changes are superficial, this indicates a response to prompting but is not evidence of self-monitoring assimilated to the subjects' knowledge about the purposes and effects of writing.

We used my error taxonomy (1981) to categorize sentence and word problems in first drafts. Recording errors in drafts and the rate of correction in revisions provided additional information on the relationship between prompting and revising.

Results

Our analyses of the subjects' writing in pen before they used Catch and after they had used it for five weeks suggest that the program stimulates changes in revising behavior, specifically, closer revising of first drafts and less rewriting. After using Catch for one month, most of the children made changes in more places in the text, but these changes involved fewer words. They made more revisions per word and slightly more types of revisions on the post-test than on the pretest, but the post-test revisions involved fewer words (297) than the pretest (417) revisions. The analysis of the types of changes made showed a higher percent of deletions on the post-test (12.7 percent of all revisions) than on the pretest (6.7 percent). Students made more substitutions and consolidations on the post-test (16.4 percent and 2.2 percent, respectively) than on the pretest (15.7 percent substitutions and no consolidations). On the other hand, they made fewer additions on the post-test (5.2 percent) than on the pretest (8.2 percent).

The number of errors per word in the pre- and post-tests suggests revising that is increasingly efficient. The children's error rates (number of word and sentence errors per word) were roughly equivalent on the pre- and post-tests (.37 and .39 errors per word, respectively). But in the post-test, the children corrected more errors (43.4 percent compared to 31.9 percent) and made fewer new ones (19.5 percent compared to 34 percent). Finally, the error rates were lower on the post-test revisions (.26) than on the pretest revisions (.35).

After using Catch, most subjects made more types of changes in their texts and corrected more errors. Five of the eight subjects' writing received higher holistic scores on the post-test than on the pretest. But few of the texts written on the computer received higher quality scores.

Case Studies and Interviews

The results reported above are based on mean scores that apply to most of the subjects. Two case studies indicated that there may be different stages of readiness for self-monitoring stimulation in writing. Janie and Randy are two young writers who responded differently to computer prompting. Janie was eleven and a half years old at the time of the experiment, and Randy was twelve and a half. Although Randy was ranked as a better writer (the best of eight) than Janie (sixth of eight), they performed equally well on a sentence memory task. Analyses of revisions stimulated by prompting and without it show that Janie revised more when Catch guided her, but Randy revised much more when he did not have prompting. In addition, Janie made more meaningful revisions (e.g., addition of clarifying information) when she used Catch. On the other hand, Randy revised more, and also more meaningfully, without external prompting.

We interviewed all the children who participated in the study. They expressed definite opinions, which usually reflected the extent to which they seemed to benefit from the programs. Five of the children found Catch to be helpful and said they would use it for all of their writing in the future if they could. Three said it helped them sometimes, and two said they would only use parts of it.

The feature the children found most helpful was "long sentences," which highlights sentences that are longer than average. The subjective report on the value of the long sentence option was supported by results from analyses of the children's writing. Seven of the children wrote shorter sentences at the end of the experimental period. Of course, short sentences are not always the best sentences; and sometimes as children shortened sentences, they created new errors, but they also corrected a higher percentage of run-on sentences.

One child felt that the long sentence option helped him find all his errors. He insisted that he did not need to use the other features if he carefully looked over the highlighted long sentences. This grand claim seems to indicate that the highlighting caused him to read more carefully than he does when all the sentences look the same. In an earlier study (1981), I found that a high percentage of many types of syntax and clarity problems occurs in sentences that are extra long. Thus, this subject may well have identified many of the problems in his text when he looked critically at those sentences, improved them, and then invented the sentences around them—as he said he did.

We also noted, however, that this subject sometimes broke up long sentences into parts and wound up with sentence fragments. We are carefully looking at this possible consequence of a long sentence identifier in our current study. Among many other analyses, we are keeping track of the occurrence of sentence fragments in the revisions of texts by subjects who use Catch and those who do not.

In our informal observations of children using Catch, we noted that they often made changes in sentences highlighted by the program but not addressed by the accompanying prompt. The options the children found overall to be most helpful were those that highlighted specific words and sentences, but we also found that the older the child, the more helpful he or she found the general prompts like "Does this paragraph have a clear focus?"

Directions for Further Study

The results from this preliminary study suggest that while children may make more changes on the computer, these changes are not always as extensive as those they make when they have to recopy. Also, when children are not guided by the computer or by another person to look closely at their drafts, they tend to rewrite and add as they revise, rather than rework what is there. We still have to determine the relative significance of these two types of revising strategies for improving writing.

As was suggested earlier, the computer has different effects for different children. Our pilot test indicated that the differences depend on the child's writing ability, which may reflect his or her cognitive development. For expert writers, differences in word processor use may depend on the writer's composing style. We will explore this possible difference for children, although we first have to determine whether apparent differences in children's approaches to writing tasks reflect different styles of working, different levels of cognitive development, or a combination of the two.

We have followed up the pilot study with a more controlled study of 70 children in the seventh, eighth, and ninth grades who wrote with computers at least once a week for one school year. Half the subjects in each grade used the word processing program and half used the word processing program and Catch. This control will indicate the differences in children who have the computer features that limit the need to recopy and those who also have the revising guide offered by Catch.

Conclusions

Children learn to use computers for writing, and they say they enjoy writing on computers more than they do with a pen. They also take to the new technology more easily than adults do. Yet, children who have written quite a bit before they use the computer work most quickly with pen and paper, even after 25 hours using the computer tools. Some of this time is taken up by typing and manipulating the cursor, and some of the time is devoted to editing while composing the draft.

Some children benefit from the computer suggestions when they return to using the pen. The children who use the computer as a guide also can say no to the superficial comments in the program as they begin to prompt themselves. These children benefit from the programs but are not dependent on them. Other children, however, benefit from computer guidance but do become dependent upon it. Thus, we have tentative evidence that a prompting program like Catch can help young writers talk to themselves about their writing, but we must still explore the relationship between children's responses to the computer and their self-initiated revising. We look forward to the research and, of course, to the results.

References

Burns, H., and G. Culp. 1980. Stimulating invention in English composition through computer-assisted instruction. *Educational Technology* 20 (Aug.): 5–10.

Collins, A. 1982. Teaching reading and writing with personal computers. National Institute of Education, Reading Syntheses Project. Typescript.

Collins, A., B. C. Bruce, and A. Rubin. 1982. Microcomputer-based writing activities for the upper elementary grades. In *Proceedings of the Fourth International Congress and Exposition of the Society for Applied Learning Technology*, Orlando, Florida.

Daiute, C. A. 1981. Psycholinguistic foundations of the writing process. *Research in the Teaching of English* 15 (Feb.): 5–22.

———. 1982. The effects of automatic prompting on young writers. Interim Report to the Spencer Foundation. Photocopy.

———. 1983. The effects of automatic prompting on young writers. Paper read at the Annual Meeting of the American Educational Research Association, Montreal.

Faigley, L., and S. Witte. 1980. Measuring the effect of revision changes on text structure. Paper read at the Annual Meeting of the National Council of Teachers of English, Cincinnati.

Kiefer, K. E., and C. R. Smith. 1983. Textual analysis with computers: Tests of Bell Laboratories' computer software. *Research in the Teaching of English* 17 (Oct.): 201–13.

Lawlor, J., ed. 1982. *Computers in composition instruction*. Los Alamitos, Calif.: SWRL Educational Research and Development.

McWilliams, P. 1982. *The word processing book*. Los Angeles: Prelude Press; distributed by Ballantine Books.

Sommers, N. 1980. Revision strategies of student writers and experienced adult writers. *College Composition and Communication* 31 (Dec.): 378–88.

IV Programs for the Writing Process

The final part of this book explores programs that integrate prewriting programs with a word processor and revising programs, thus facilitating all stages of the writing process. Chapter 10 details how a series of prewriting programs grew to include a word processor and revision programs. Chapter 11 describes WANDAH, UCLA's program for all stages of the writing process. In Chapter 12 Cynthia Selfe explains her series of programs intended to help with writing in the various rhetorical modes. The final chapter of the collection describes how faculty at Carnegie-Mellon University are creating an integrated prewriting-writing-revising program.

10 Questions, Answers, and Automated Writing

William Wresch
University of Wisconsin Center, Marinette

As a junior college English teacher for two or three eternities, one of the things that has always bothered me about much of the student writing I see is lack of organization and development. I know there are others who are driven crazy by grammar and those who retire early because they can't bear to see one more *alot*. But my concern has been the countless papers that wander all over the map without making any attempt at supporting or explaining any of the ten or twelve thousand assertions made per page.

There are of course a number of ways of dealing with this problem short of career change. After taking several computer science courses, it occurred to me that the computer might provide one more means. I started with a simple program that asked a number of questions, stored the answers, and then reformatted the answers according to whether a cause/effect, comparison, or descriptive organization was preferred. It looked pretty jazzy since the program could instantly "write" three different essays on the same subject at the push of a button, but it was really just a gimmick. It did, however, get me thinking along the lines of questioning students, saving their answers, and then showing them how that information could be put into a coherent framework.

About this time the Apple Education Foundation gave me some computing equipment in return for which I promised to produce a program that would do everything, including write on water. I wrote a rough version of a program I called Essaywriter early in the grant period and tried it on my students. Essentially the program called on students to pick a subject, choose whether to describe the subject's job, appearance, history, or causes, pick the six major features of the job, appearance, etc., select the three most important ones, and then write six sentences explaining each of the three major features. The result was the standard five-paragraph theme; each of the three features served as a topic sentence for a paragraph, with the six sentences of description used as the paragraph body. The program generated an introduction and some transitions, and an essay of sorts was automatically written. (For a more complete description see Wresch [1983].)

After a class had gone through the program, it was much easier to talk to them about topic sentences and forms of support and elaboration, but as a real essay writer, the program still had some problems. One was that it was written for the old Apple II Plus which could generate only capital letters. Another was that the program had no way to allow spelling corrections and even minor rewriting. I knew that if the program was going to be more than an exercise, if it was actually going to produce a rough draft of an organized and supported essay for a student to flesh out, it would have to be tied to a word processor.

About this time, I met many of the others who were working on computer-assisted writing. I was impressed with some of the approaches they were taking and decided to incorporate (i.e., steal) many of their ideas. From Hugh Burns, I learned ways to expand the questioner. From Ray Rodrigues, I learned to offer different prewriting activities so students could choose whichever worked best for them. From Mike Cohen, Ruth Von Blum, Kate Kiefer, Charles Smith, and Colette Daiute, I learned some of the possible computerized responses to student writing that had worked successfully. Taking these ideas, my need for an integrated word processor, and my experience with Essaywriter, I put together Writer's Helper.

Writer's Helper is essentially three groups of programs. The first group contains nearly a dozen prewriting programs, the second is a specially designed word processor, and the last group contains several programs to analyze student essays.

The Prewriter

Prewriting programs received most of my efforts. I know it is hard to get students to use prewriting activities outside of class, and even English teachers tend to go comatose when the subject comes up. But I've always felt the only way to avoid correctly spelled drivel was to prewrite and prewrite and prewrite some more.

Writer's Helper approaches prewriting through levels, options, and electronic gimmickry. It uses levels because students come with different prewriting needs. Some just need to explore a subject, while others have no idea which subject to choose. The program has options that allow students to select more than one prewriting activity at each level. It has gimmickry in that for each activity, I have tried to ask what the computer could do that a workbook couldn't. In some cases it was random feedback; in others it was storing and reformatting student answers.

Students select from levels and options through menus. The first menu they see lists the four levels at which they can work:

```
1) Find a subject

2) Explore a subject

3) Organize information about a subject

4) Develop a single paragraph
```

The focus of each level is pretty obvious. Let's look briefly at each.

If students choose number one, the screen displays three options for them: BRAINSTORMS, LISTS, or THE QUESTIONER. BRAINSTORMS is an automated freewriting activity. It differs from normal freewriting because the program contains a timer that will start automatically typing X's if students take more than a second between keystrokes. Obviously, this is no exercise for nontypists (and students are told this), but it will nudge along those who otherwise miss the point of freewriting and poke along.

LISTS asks for words or phrases to be typed in, then displays them on the computer screen followed by random comments such as "That's interesting," "Nice idea." It leads students to choose one idea from a list, write a list about that idea, choose one from that list and use it to create another list, until students have found a subject or grown tired of the approach.

THE QUESTIONER is a series of 20 questions, such as "Whom do you most admire?" and "What makes you most proud of your school?" intended to start students thinking about a range of subjects from the most personal to the fairly abstract. It also supplies random feedback to students.

The assumption behind the three approaches is that each will at least appeal to some students and that each will at least help students with the preliminary task of finding a general subject. Should a student already have a subject in mind but need to develop it, he or she has the option to select Explore a Subject. This level also has three options: CRAZY CONTRASTS, TREES, and THREE WAYS OF SEEING.

CRAZY CONTRASTS is a direct steal from Ray Rodrigues. The program asks students to type in a subject and then randomly selects one of 20 unusual contrasting subjects. That contrasting subject is displayed and students are asked to list four ways their subject is like "day-old bread" or "a parking meter," then list three reasons their friends might see the subject as similar to "an English muffin" or "Richard Nixon." Students can quit the program anytime, but as long as they ask it to, the computer will keep juxtaposing unusual contrasts with their subject, leading them, I hope, to new insights on the subject.

TREES asks students to name a subject and then list 15 related ideas, objects, or people. The program helps students find general categories for items in the list and then automatically generates and displays a tree structure with the subject as the trunk, categories as branches, and the 15 items as twigs on the various branches. The idea of course is to help students look for general groupings of ideas within their assorted opinions.

THREE WAYS OF SEEING is a lengthy questioner that asks students to name a subject and then follows the general lines of the Young, Becker, and Pike approach, asking about the subject in isolation, as part of a process, and as part of a network. In this, as in all the other activities, the student is not only asked questions but is told the purpose for the approach and the results that can reasonably be expected.

The third prewriter level a student may choose is the organizational. At this level the student presumably has chosen a subject and explored it and now is looking for help in organizing ideas. The program is essentially the earlier Essaywriter recast in light of suggestions (and complaints) I have received over the last year. It begins by asking students to type in a subject and select one of six purposes:

```
1) Describe the appearance of the
   subject

2) Compare the subject to another
   subject
```

```
3) Show how the subject has changed over
   time

4) Describe the job or function of the
   subject

5) Show what caused the subject to be
   the way it is now

6) Describe the importance of the
   subject
```

After selecting one of these purposes, students are asked to identify an audience for their essay; then they are asked about that audience's opinion of the subject. For instance, if a student says her or his purpose is to describe the appearance of a friend, the program asks if the given audience would agree that the friend's appearance was unique, hard to imagine, or not so unusual. The program's purpose is to get students writing to a specific audience and thinking in advance of that audience's opinions. The next question asked is whether the writer shares that opinion. If so, the goal is to say something that will hold the audience's attention; if not, the goal is to change the audience's mind.

With a subject, audience, and purpose clearly in the student's mind, the program asks him or her for sentences of support, organizes the sentences into paragraphs with topic and body paragraphs, and prints out a rough essay. In the example below, a subject, Teachers, and goal, "Describe the job or function," have already been selected. The transcript picks up at the point of audience identification.

```
Name your audience: Ronald Reagan

Good. Now let's think a little about
what kinds of opinions Ronald Reagan
already has about the job or function of
Teachers.

If you asked Ronald Reagan about the job
or function of Teachers, which of these
statements do you think he would most
likely agree with?
```

    1) the job or function of teachers is
       unique.
    2) the job or function of teachers is
       hard to imagine.
    3) the job or function of teachers is
       not so difficult.

<u>3</u>

What do YOU think? Do you agree with
your audience? Type in a ''yes'' or a
''no'' and press RETURN.

<u>no</u>

Good. You can explain to your audience
why they are wrong. You may have to
supply some convincing proof, but this
should be an interesting essay for them
to read.

Start by listing 3 aspects of the job or
functions of teachers which are more
difficult than most people think.

    1) <u>inspiring learning</u>
    2) <u>maintaining discipline</u>
    3) <u>maintaining morale</u>

Now let's describe those parts of the
job or function of teachers that you
said were more difficult than most
people think.

The parts you listed were
    1) inspiring learning
    2) maintaining discipline
    3) maintaining morale
To begin with, you said that teachers'

inspiring learning is more difficult
than most people think. Type in 4
complete sentences which would help show
that to your audience.
    1) Students often come from homes
where learning isn't valued.
    2) A father who earns more with a high
school education than a teacher with a
college education isn't likely to praise
school.
    3) Television also portrays school as
a place where learning is secondary.
    4) It seems like only troubled kids
get any attention.

This is repeated for each of the other two paragraphs.

Good work. You now have taken three
parts of the job or function of teachers
and tried to show how each of them is
more difficult than most people think. I
showed you how your supporting sentences
might be put together in a paragraph.
Now let me show you how all of what you
told me could be put together to form an
essay.
                    Teachers
    Most people think that the job or
function of teachers is not so
difficult. But that really isn't true.
Here are three places where the job or
function of teachers is more difficult
than most people think.

    One part of the job or function of
teachers that is more difficult than
most people think is inspiring learning.
Students often come from homes where

learning isn't valued. A father who earns more with a high school education than a teacher with a college education isn't likely to praise school. Television also portrays school as a place where learning is secondary. It seems only troubled kids get any attention.

Another part of the job or function of teachers that is more difficult than most people think is maintaining discipline. Principals sometimes don't support their teachers. Rules are often unevenly enforced. Parents often don't support teachers. Discipline is breaking down all over—why not schools too?

The third part of the job or function of teachers that is more difficult than most people think is maintaining morale. Teachers are called professionals but can't even pick their own texts. Every pay raise is put on the front page of the paper. Articles also claim new teachers are dumb. When some teachers leave the profession those who stay behind feel like leftovers.

So there shouldn't be much doubt. Because of inspiring learning and maintaining discipline and maintaining morale it is clear the job or function of teachers is really more difficult than most people think.

How's that for an essay? Pretty rough, isn't it? But it does show you one way your ideas about teachers could be organized.

The program goes on to explain the process it used and to ask the student if she or he wants to save the essay on a disk so it can be modified on the word processor or printed on the printer.

The last of the four prewriting levels is Develop a single paragraph. This program takes students through paragraph construction using details, examples, or statistics for support. It can be used independently, but it is really intended to be used as an aid to students who have been told by the analysis section that one of their paragraphs may be weak. But more on that later.

The Word Processor

Early on, I saw a need for a word processor to tie into many of my prewriting modules. My choices were to use a commercial program and hope to modify the output of the prewriting programs so files could be interchanged or to write a word processor of my own. A commercial word processor would have been the easier choice, but it would also have meant constantly changing disks and added expense if anyone off campus wanted to use my prewriting programs. So with more courage than sense, I hired a student of mine and set out to create a word processor that would work with my other programs and also eliminate some of the shortcomings I saw in available processors.

Three months later, I had a processor I could live with. It takes full advantage of the Apple IIe's standard 80-column card to produce sharp upper- and lowercase characters and uses menu layouts across the top of the screen much like Bank Street Writer and WordStar, two processors I wish I had written. Other than that, my program is pretty much a generic word processor that happens to interface nicely with my other Writer's Helper programs and resides on the same disk with them for convenience.

The Analyzer

I have worked on computer-assisted writing programs for several years now and have avoided automatic feedback programs until very recently. At first I stayed away because I was more interested in prewriting approaches; then I stayed away because, like many others, I was concerned by their weaknesses. You know the concern. What would Writer's Workbench or Grammatik say to Faulkner: Shorten your sentences? Use fewer prepositions? Be less parenthetical?

Despite my concerns, I finally decided to write some programs that would analyze some aspects of student writing. I did so because I saw that such programs give useful, if limited, information to students about their work, they create new opportunities for teachers to discuss elements of style they normally can't interest students in, and they are fun. These are the six analysis programs I finally wrote:

1. Homonym checker
2. Outliner
3. Readability level
4. Sentence graph
5. Paragraph development
6. Usage checker

Should students desire feedback on an essay they have produced in the word processor or in the PREWRITER essay generator, they ask the computer to run the analyzer program and the above menu appears. They can get as much or as little reaction to their essay as they care to simply by typing in the number of the form of analysis they prefer.

HOMONYM CHECKER goes through students' essays looking for the dreaded *to, too,* and *two* as well as other commonly confused homonyms. In the case of clear errors such as *should of* or *alot,* the error is marked and the correct spelling printed out. In the case of *there, their,* and *they're,* the program points out the correct usage of each and lets students decide if they have used the word correctly.

OUTLINER prints out the first sentence of each paragraph and asks students to check for transitions and logical sequence. READABILITY LEVEL asks students to estimate the reading level of their audience. It then calculates the level of the student essay and compares the two. Suggestions for bringing the essay more into line with the audience are then given.

SENTENCE GRAPH was stolen directly from Michael Cohen's HOMER. It depicts sentences by printing one star for each word in the sentence. The result is a graph that quickly shows the length and variety of sentences used. PARAGRAPH DEVELOPMENT graphs paragraphs rather than sentences. If it finds short paragraphs, it suggests they might lack development and directs the student to the paragraph development section of the PREWRITER program. USAGE CHECKER searches a student essay for *affect* and *effect* and the like and explains how each is commonly used. It is up to the writer to determine if the essay usage is correct.

Some of these analysis programs such as the homonym and usage checkers are designed to be of direct use to students and should cut down on the number of such errors teachers see. Other programs such as the sentence and paragraph graphers can be useful alone but should be more beneficial as classroom discussion starters. When should sentences be short? Long? Why a variety? And then there is the element of fun. Why not have the computer graph your essay or compute its readability level?

I have seen a room full of English teachers really enjoy themselves for over an hour writing paragraphs and then waiting to see what kind of readability level would be computed for their efforts. If such feedback will generate writing and thinking about writing, why not use it?

Classroom Use

By its very nature, Writer's Helper is designed to be used independently by students outside of class. Because of this, I make its use optional. At the beginning of each semester, I take each of my classes into the micro-computer lab and show them how to use the word processor and access the prewriting and analyzer programs. Once they have seen what these programs can do and how they are used, I leave it up to the students to decide whether or not to use the programs. Generally, one-third will use the program from the very beginning, one-third will use it as the semester progresses, and one-third will never return to the computer room.

While Writer's Helper is used as an option and independently, that does not mean it is extraneous to the classroom. I use the program's prewriting activities in class. Analysis areas the program checks I also check and discuss in class. I talk to students about information they get from the computer and uses they can make of the computer. Obviously, Writer's Helper would be better integrated into the classroom routine if it were a required component of the course, but there are enough cyberphobes out there that I am uncomfortable about making such a requirement.

Writer's Helper is currently being field tested at the University of California, Berkeley, Harvard University, and New Mexico State, as well as at a number of high schools. During the 1984–85 school year, it will be formally studied as it is used extensively in the Arlington Heights, Illinois, middle schools. High school and college teachers who have used the program so far find that students respond well to it, and the teachers themselves find it easily fits within their writing curriculum.

System Requirements

Writer's Helper runs on an Apple IIe with one disk drive and an 80-column card. This is the configuration Apple refers to as its "startup system." A printer is recommended but need not be hooked up to each computer running the program.

Program Availability

Writer's Helper is available from CONDUIT, University of Iowa-Oakdale Campus, Iowa City, Iowa 52242.

11 WANDAH: Writing-Aid AND Author's Helper

Ruth Von Blum
Michael E. Cohen
University of California, Los Angeles

Two lines of research, one basic and one applied, make us think that computers might usefully aid writers. The first, cognitive process research, examines in detail the mechanisms people use to solve complex problems. This research sees writing as a complex problem-solving task, not unlike scientific or mathematical problem solving, and it helps explain specific difficulties that student writers encounter. The second line of research explores how computers may intervene by providing specific writer's aids.

A writer must attend to a number of tasks simultaneously, tasks that range from syntax, spelling, grammar, and handwriting to generating ideas, integrating these ideas into a coherent framework, and considering rhetorical purpose and audience. Some of these tasks are more complex than others. But writers must simultaneously perform *all* of the cognitive tasks constituting the writing process, both the trivial and the complex. The inexperienced writer, especially, can easily become overburdened.

Good writers have made the more trivial tasks routine. These writers may, for example, make grammar and punctuation choices more or less automatically. They can then concentrate more readily on the higher order writing tasks, such as developing ideas and organizing their presentation. Less accomplished writers have no such luxury. Grammatical and mechanical concerns compete with organizational and stylistic considerations, leaving the writer floundering and frustrated. Obviously, effective writing instruction must help remove the "writer's overload" so that student writers may concentrate on the structure and arrangement of their ideas.

WANDAH was developed by the Word Processor Writing Project; Morton Friedman and Earl Rand, principal investigators; Ruth Von Blum, project director; Michael Cohen, principal programmer. The project was funded by a grant from the Exxon Education Foundation.

Cognitive process research has examined not only *what* writers do when they write but *when* they do it. The research shows that good writers revise their work continuously—and at several levels—as they compose. Poor writers do not. This failure to revise is especially important, because neither poor nor good writers spend much time consciously planning the shape and organization of their written work (Emig 1971; Bereiter 1979). A major difference, therefore, between good and poor writers comes as they commit words to paper. Good writers plan and revise as they go along, while poor writers write without self-monitoring feedback (Hayes and Flower 1979).

This line of research, then, led us to believe that mediation to help reduce the writer's cognitive burden and to encourage revision would improve writing. We thought that the computerized word processor might provide such help. Since word processors greatly facilitate editing and revising, we reasoned that such programs might, in and of themselves, provide a powerful aid to student writing. The word processor may also help alleviate some of the student writer's cognitive burden. Since errors can be corrected so easily, students may concentrate more on the ideas and their organization when they compose. In addition, they can focus attention on one writing problem at a time—writing first for ideas and going through subsequent drafts to revise for word choice, grammar, punctuation, spelling, etc. The word processor might thus encourage revision. Some preliminary studies of students composing with word processors do indeed show improvement in certain kinds of revision (Daiute 1983; see also Chapter 9 of this book).

Computers may intervene more directly, as indicated by a second line of research. Several computer-assisted instruction programs help students in the prewriting and revising stages, as well as in the actual composing stage. Prewriting aids that help unblock students and encourage them to "get it down, even if they do not get it right" have been adapted for the computer (Schwartz 1982; Burns and Culp 1980; see also Chapters 1 and 3). These generally prompt students to answer specific questions about their topics and to "brainstorm" with the computer.

At the other end of the writing process, a number of currently available programs help revise text once it has been written. Some of these, like HOMER (Cohen 1982; see also Chapter 5), can point out stylistic problems. Others point out possible spelling, punctuation, or similar mechanical errors. Research shows that such programs can help students write. For example, students using the Writer's Workbench, a Bell Laboratories program originally designed to improve technical writing, revised their papers as recommended by the programs (Kiefer 1982; see also Chapter 4).

Research on the Limits of Computerized Writing Aids

Unfortunately, most word processors are devices for *transcription*, not *creation*, of text. They were designed for office use, and the bulk of the commands assist with formatting text. Because these commands tend to be complex, they can make learning to use the system extremely difficult. In addition, most systems assume that the user is a well-trained operator (usually a secretary) who can afford considerable time to learn the system and who uses it continuously. Finally, because these word processors assume that the text has been created elsewhere and that it is merely being transcribed by an individual other than the author, they do not have special features that might be valuable for the writer.

Some preliminary research investigating the effect of word processors on writing points out the difficulty students have learning to use the computer (Collier 1983; Nancarrow 1983). These problems may cause a new kind of cognitive overload, increasing the difficulties already experienced by less competent writers. Other effects are more subtle but ultimately may be more important. Composing with a word processor means interacting with a new medium, and this may present its own difficulties. We had expected that students would revise more frequently and that their revisions would be more at the level of ideas when they used the word processor. Recent research indicates that students may indeed revise more frequently, but that the bulk of it is surface revision. We can speculate this is partly because the writer cannot see more than a small portion of the paper at any one time (usually only 24 lines). Large-scale revisions, including several paragraphs or pages, become even more difficult to conceptualize than they would by using pencil, paper, and scissors to cut and paste.

Furthermore, some students produce more rambling papers that are noticeably *less* well organized than their usual written work precisely because it is so easy to type away using a word processor without the usual concerns about errors in style and mechanics. These students then have difficulty paring down and organizing their work. Also, because the word processor prints out clean drafts with a finished appearance, students may be less inclined to view the work as in progress and therefore may be less likely to want to change it significantly. Some very preliminary observations that we made of students writing with word processors indicate that these problems may affect good as well as poor writers.

In addition, research points out that students try to preserve their own writing and revising styles, regardless of the injection of the word processor into the process. Thus, students who tend to revise mostly at the surface level will continue to do so (perhaps even more), while students who routinely revise on several levels will try to use the word processor in a manner consistent with their own writing styles. But most word processors are not easily adapted to varying writing styles; even more importantly, they do not guide students to significantly revise their work.

Purpose of the Word Processor Writing Project

We were convinced that an *integrated* computerized writer's aid system could significantly improve student writing. The Word Processor Writing Project, funded by a grant from the Exxon Education Foundation, has developed such a comprehensive word processor-based system for improving composition. The system, called WANDAH (Writing-Aid AND Author's Helper), has three major components:

1. A word processor designed expressly for on-line composing.
2. A set of computerized prewriting aids to encourage planning and the free flow of ideas.
3. A set of aids to facilitate reviewing and revising the work thematically, stylistically, and grammatically.

The figure labeled WANDAH Overview depicts the program components.

We designed the WANDAH system specifically to help university-level students in first-year writing classes. We based the design on a set of assumptions about the nature of the composing process, the ways in which the computer can most efficiently help students write, and the particular circumstances under which students will most likely use the program. We can summarize these as follows: (1) Composing is problem solving with words. It is a complex, recursive process calling upon many disparate cognitive skills. (2) Computers can help students at all stages of the writing process—prewriting, writing, and revising—and can reduce the cognitive burden at each stage. (3) Students will use the system as part of classroom instruction in first-year composition. This, we assume, means students who are largely inexperienced with computers and with word processing; equally (or more) inexperienced teachers; a limited number of computers in the classroom; limited time available to learn to use the system; and intermittent use by each student throughout the course (meaning potential problems with having to relearn the system each time it is used).

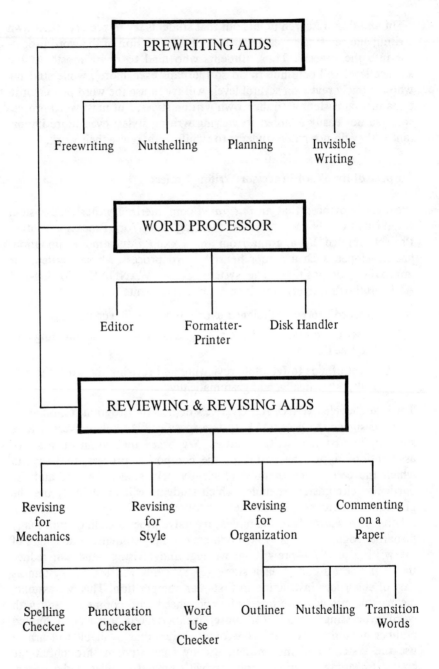

WANDAH Overview. The integrated program, built around the word processor, provides assistance to the writing process.

Description of WANDAH

The system was essentially complete as of March 1984. Features of the system may change as a result of testing. Thus, the version finally distributed may differ from the one described here.

The Word Processor

A powerful yet friendly word processor designed to facilitate composing, as contrasted with transcribing, is the heart of the WANDAH system. It is a full-screen text editor; students can move the cursor (a flashing underline) anywhere on the screen and can alter the text. Several features make the word processor easy to use. WANDAH has a tutorial that teaches students how to use the word processor. Students work through a set of activities, practicing as they go along, to learn the basic features of the word processor (this takes around one hour). After practicing with the system, they then return for a few additional lessons that teach the more advanced features. The program itself uses an elaborate menu system. As shown below, students need not remember what keys to press to get around the system.

```
                WANDAH'S WORD PROCESSOR
                      MAIN MENU

      (L) LEARN to use this Word Processor

      (W) WRITE/WORK ON a paper

      (P) PRINT a paper

      (E) ERASE/RENAME/COPY a paper

      (R) READY a disk to receive papers

      <BACK> Main Menu of WANDAH System

      (Q) QUIT the system

   Your Selection Please: _
```

WANDAH offers extensive prompts on the screen. The next example shows the screen as it normally appears, with all of the available functions indicated in the second line, called the command line.

```
Paper: LESSON1 Date Created: 6/28
Version #5
<BACK> <COPY> <ERASE> <HELP> <INSERT>
<SEARCH> <TIDY> <1/2 SCRN>
.pb:
(The WANDAH user's manual will tell the
teacher how to set up the computer and
the printer and how to format disks. We
assume here that the student is sitting
in front of a fully functional WANDAH
station.):
:
:
.ce:
WANDAH'S WORD PROCESSOR TUTORIAL--
LESSON 1:
:
:
WHAT IS A WORD PROCESSOR? :
:
A word processor is a computer program
that lets you type, edit, and format
text easily and conveniently. After you
SAVE your paper (explained in Lesson 2),
it is stored on your PAPERS disk. You
can retrieve it, edit it, and store the
revised version, as well as printing out
various versions, thus eliminating the
need for extensive retyping. We designed
WANDAH's word processor to help you
compose and revise papers directly at
the computer.:
:
:
LEARNING TO USE WANDAH'S WORD PROCESSOR:
```

When the student is using any special function, such as **COPY** or **SEARCH**, messages appear that guide the student through each step of the process. On-line help is provided when requested. The following simulated display shows a typical help screen.

```
           ADDING (INSERTING) TEXT

On a BLANK screen or at END of text --
Just TYPE, (<UNTYPE> erases).
When you are OVER text -- Just TYPE over
the text. <UNTYPE> will restore previous
characters.
BETWEEN letters -- Press <INSERT>. Text
will ''open up.'' Type insert of any
length. <UNTYPE> erases, press <BACK>
when done.

CARRIAGE RETURNS AUTOMATICALLY. Press
<RETURN> to FORCE end of line,
marked '':''
   <BACK> to previous activity
(W) Write/Edit Menu

   Paper: LESSON1 Date Created: 6/28
   Version #5
<BACK> <COPY> <ERASE> <HELP> <INSERT>
<SEARCH> <TIDY> <1/2 SCRN> <OTHR SCRN>
.pb:
(The WANDAH user's manual will tell the
teacher how to set up the computer and
the printer and how to format disks. We
assume here that the student is sitting
in front of a fully functional WANDAH
station.):
:
:
.ce:
WANDAH'S WORD PROCESSOR TUTORIAL --
LESSON 1:
```

When the student presses the HELP key, the screen splits in half horizontally, and a help menu appears. The student simply selects the type of help and a message appears. This message remains on the screen as long as needed and can then be cleared. In addition, a sheet of cardboard, to be placed near the keyboard, provides a guide to the most common word processor functions.

Special function keys are another important feature of the system. Novice or intermittent users of word processors find it much easier to use the system if each activity they have to do is controlled by a special, labeled key. Thus, we have clustered the ten cursor movement keys on the left side of the keyboard and the other special function keys on the right. Each key is clearly labeled, and in those cases where a key needs to serve more than one function, the functions are closely related. For example, pressing the <WORD> key moves the cursor one word to the right, and pressing it while also holding down the <REVERSE> key moves the cursor one word to the left.

One of the chief fears of new word processor users is that their work will somehow disappear. This is indeed a justified fear with many word processors! WANDAH's word processor has a number of features to help prevent such disasters. Students may recover erasures via the <RESTORE> key. This is a sort of "oops" key that, when pressed immediately after an erasure, will return the erased text to the screen. If an erasure is too large to be restored (over 750 words), the student is warned before the erasure is completed. In addition, erasures of more than one paragraph require confirmation. The command line states the number of lines that are about to be erased, and the student must confirm the choice. Lastly, after the student leaves an editing session, a menu appears. The student cannot forget to SAVE the paper; a specific choice must be made either to SAVE the paper, RENAME it, or THROW IT AWAY. If the latter option is chosen, the student must confirm the choice by a two-keystroke action. If SAVE is selected and a previous version of the paper is already on the disk, the student must again specifically request to SAVE the screen version and to write over the one already on disk. (Choosing the RENAME option is the way to save multiple versions of the same paper.)

WANDAH's word processor also simplifies printing papers, erasing papers from the disk, copying papers to other disks, and preparing disks to receive papers. A menu guides students through each of these activities. The word processor provides only those formatting commands for the printer that are most useful for student essay writing. Students type in special commands for the printer within their texts (on separate lines). These commands are printed on the summary and can also be accessed by pressing the <HELP> key. Before WANDAH begins printing the paper, it shows the "default" values upon which the printer operates, for instance, one-inch margins at the right and bottom, one and a half inches at the left and top of the page, automatic page numbering, and double spacing. The student may easily change any of these options or, by simply pressing the <P> key, begin printing.

WANDAH features make composing at the computer especially easy and productive. The student may "split the screen." When the <1/2 SCREEN> key is pressed, the screen splits in two horizontally. This lets the student display another paper or an outline on the second screen and keep it there for reference. The student may also split the screen on the paper currently being edited, allowing simultaneous comparisons of two text portions. He or she can move freely between the two screens by pressing the <OTHER SCREEN> key and can edit whichever paper the cursor is on. The student may also copy text from one screen to the other, making it especially easy to move around large blocks of text. This feature also lets the student start new papers very easily. If one paper is too large to be handled in one file, the student simply splits the screen and begins a "new" paper (actually a continuation of the current paper) on the other screen. The following simulated display shows a split screen.

```
Analysis of YUCKSTY for      Words=111
''Be'' verbs, Prepositions    Sentences=6

Word processors greatly increase the
ease of editing and revision.  Words,
sentences, paragraphs, and even whole
pages of text can be moved about quickly
and with a minimum of effort.  Routine
correction of typing errors; insertions
and deletion of words, sentences, and
paragraphs; and production of final
formatted copy can all be done quickly
and easily.  Clean copies of rough
drafts can be printed out with wide
margins and ample spacing between lines
for pencilled insertions and
corrections.  Word processors relieve
the writer from trivial aspects of the
writing process.  Thus, students using a
```

```
word processor will be relatively free
to concentrate on the structure,
organization, and content of their
essays.

be=''Be'' verbs; p=Prepositions


____ _____ _____ _____ ____ __
____ pp _____ ___ _____.  _____,
_____,  _____,  ___ ____ ____
_____ pp ____ ___ bb _____ ppppp _____
___ pppp _ _____ pp _____.  _____
_____ pp _____ _ _____;  _____
___ _____ pp _____,  _____,  ___
_____;  ___ _____ pp ____
_____ ___ ____ __ ___ _____ _____
___ _____.  _____ _____ pp ____
_____ ___ bb _____ ___ pppp _____
_____ ___ ___ _____ _____ pppppp _____
ppp _____ _____ ___
_____.  ___ _____ ____ _____
___ _____ pppp _____ _____ ___ pp __
____ ___ _____.  ____,  _____ ____ __
____ _____ ____ bb _____ ___
pp _____ pp ___ _____,
_____,  ___ _____ pp _____
_____.
```

Cursor moves are partially syntactic. The cursor moves by word, sentence, and paragraph (forward and backward) as well as by character, screen page, and to the beginning or end of a line or of the paper. Erasures and the copy command also use these same units. Thus, the student may be more inclined to think of revising on the sentence and paragraph level when it is so easy to manipulate these syntactic units.

The printing part of the word processor lets the student get quick "draft prints" of the paper in progress. These prints may be single-, double-, or triple-spaced; they are identical to the way the text appears on the screen, including the location of forced carriage returns (when the student pressed the <RETURN> key) and imbedded printer commands.

The screen does *not* reformat as the student edits. The text on some word processors is in almost constant motion as words are added or deleted, an annoying distraction for those composing at the computer. WANDAH's word processor "opens up" when text is inserted, the location of the cursor is marked by a slash, and the remainder of the line moves to the bottom of the screen. When the insert is completed, the text closes up again. Small erasures cause only the current line to reformat. For larger erasures, the entire screen blanks out momentarily and then is redisplayed. Any extra spaces left on the screen are automatically eliminated by the printer. Simply pressing the <TIDY> key "tidies up" the paragraph upon which the cursor rests and removes any extra spaces from the display screen.

Since typing on a word processor is so easy for many students, simple typographical errors are common. The word processor has automatic typeover so that the student merely moves the cursor to the error and types in the correction without having to erase it first. Once characters have been typed over, they can be restored by pressing the <UNTYPE> key. Also, to add to the end of existing text, the student merely goes to the end of the text and continues typing. There is no need to enter a special insert mode at this point. Erasures are also easy to make using a special <ERASE> key that, when pressed at the same time as a cursor movement key, erases a specified amount of text. For example, <ERASE> with <WORD> erases the word under the cursor and the following space.

Finally, both searching through the text to find particular words and copying portions of the text from one place to another are extremely easy to do with this word processor. They are activities initiated with a single keystroke and guided every step of the way.

Prewriting Aids

Students can access the prewriting aids at any time while writing. We specifically present a choice of aids, knowing that different techniques are appropriate for different students' styles of writing and different teachers' styles of teaching. WANDAH offers four prewriting aids.

Nutshelling

Based on an idea of Linda Flower's (1981), nutshelling asks the student to type in the purpose and audience of the paper plus a brief summary of its main ideas—in other words, to "put it in a nutshell." This encourages the student to think in broad terms about the rhetorical purpose of the work and to begin formulating a strategy for attacking the writing problem. The student creates a "nutshell statement" that is then stored on the disk.

This statement can later be edited like any paper, and the student may actually build the paper around the nutshell statement by inserting text. Students are encouraged to save the nutshell statement in its original form for comparison with a similar statement made after a draft of the paper is done.

Invisible Writing

The idea for invisible writing was drawn from work done by Stephen Marcus (1983) at the South Coast Writing Project and also from observations made by several colleagues and one of the authors who regularly compose on word processors. One of the greatest difficulties for many writers is overcoming the urge to edit each line as it is composed. This problem very well may be exacerbated when composing on the computer since editing is so much easier (and less messy). The problem is compounded when the writing is not going smoothly; editing existing text provides activity for a mind frustrated by its inability to continue writing. At these times, turning off the screen so that the writer cannot see the text can help unblock the writing process. Since the writer cannot rely on looking at the actual words, ideas must be kept constantly in mind, as must the structure of the argument being presented. The writer cannot edit what is being written and must simply plow ahead—trying to "get it down, even it if is not just right." The strategy runs counter to the belief of many students that the text must be perfect the moment it is created.

A student requests this prewriting aid from the menu and is told to type away. If desired, an outline for a nutshell statement may be on one screen for reference. After typing at least 100 words, the student is given the option to see what has been written. She or he then may continue writing invisibly or may save the work on the disk like any paper; the student can later request it from WANDAH's word processor and edit or add to it in the normal fashion.

Freewriting

Using ideas popularized by Peter Elbow (1973), the freewriting program, structurally similar to invisible writing, lets students see what they write but urges them to keep typing without pause. The screen blinks if a student stops writing for more than a few seconds. Students may not correct errors or edit while they are freewriting. After they have finished with the exercise, they may save and then edit or expand their work.

Planning

The planning aid asks the student for the title and main idea (thesis) of the paper; it then asks for arguments supporting it and possible counter-arguments. Once the student has supplied these, the program allows the student to select and organize these arguments into a coherent outline for the paper.

Reviewing and Revising Aids

Once the student has created some text, whether a complete draft or only a portion, he or she can subject it to one of the three sets of reviewing and revising aids.

Revising for Mechanics

The mechanics aid is actually three separate programs, each of which processes the text and highlights common surface problems

Punctuation. The punctuation program identifies unpaired parentheses, quotation marks, and brackets, as well as possibly incorrect placement of punctuation (periods, commas, etc.) within quotation marks and parentheses. It also tells the student when a question mark may be missing from the end of the sentence. More difficult problems, such as correct placement of commas within the syntactic structure of the text, are beyond the capabilities of this program.

Word usage. The usage program highlights any words that might be a potential usage problem. The student may then request a one-line explanation of the possible difficulty. For example, the words *accept* or *except* would be highlighted and explained as follows: "Accept: to receive with consent; except: excluding." The words *its* and *it's* would be accompanied by the message, "its: possessive pronoun; it's: contraction for it is." The program has stored over 100 such words with accompanying messages.

Spelling checker. The spelling program simply checks all the words in the text against a stored dictionary and informs the student that unrecognized words may be misspelled.

Revising for Style

The style aid helps students see certain stylistic features of their texts: abstract words, prepositional phrases, selected gender-specific (and possibly sexist) nouns, *be* verbs, and possible nominalizations. It also provides an analysis of sentence length and paragraph length. Like the Writer's Workbench, HOMER, Grammatik, and other computerized stylistic analyses, WANDAH's style aid only spots rough surface features. Stylistic features with a large semantic component (e.g., dangling modifiers) do not lend themselves easily to computer analysis.

Students first choose the paper they wish to analyze. WANDAH then lets them pick which of the five possible word types they wish to see isolated in the analysis. Students may choose any combination of the five.

Once the choice has been made, WANDAH splits the screen and begins displaying the analysis.

The top screen presents the paper's text much as it appeared in the word processor but with one change: WANDAH highlights words belonging to any of the selected word types. The bottom screen displays a graphic representation of the top screen, where underscores represent the nonhighlighted words and a sequence of letters (e.g., an *a* for an abstract word) represents a word belonging to one of the selected word types. WANDAH also displays a running total of words and sentences in the upper righthand corner of the screen. The simulated split-screen display earlier in this chapter shows a style analysis of prepositions and *be* verbs.

When WANDAH finishes displaying the analysis, students may see a statistical summary of the analysis. For example, students may see the average number of words per sentence and per paragraph and the average number of prepositions per sentence. WANDAH also adds prose comments that may alert the student to possible problems. We've phrased those comments as gentle reminders rather than authoritative dicta, since the program has no insight into meaning. Students are free to ignore comments that they deem inappropriate. Like the rest of WANDAH's writing aids, the style aid works best when students have discussed the issues it addresses in class.

Revising for Organization

The organization aids may be the most significant of the reviewing and revising programs. They try to overcome some of the organization problems that may be made worse by students' composing at the word processor. There are three organization aids.

Nutshelling. Similar to the prewriting aid, this nutshelling program asks the student to wait at least half a day after finishing a draft before writing the nutshell statement and to do so without looking at what has been written. The student is then prompted to compare this nutshell with what actually appears in the text and with any prewriting nutshell or outline.

Overview summary outline. WANDAH presents two outline options. The student may either receive an outline made up of the first sentence in each paragraph, or the student may pick one sentence out of each paragraph that best presents the main idea of the paragraph. The reason for the option is obvious: the first sentence of a paragraph is often not the topic sentence nor should it necessarily be. Such outlines help the student see the general progression of the paper's main ideas.

Transition words. The transitions aid highlights selected transition words and phrases and/or pronouns, thus encouraging the student to consider whether the paper contains smooth transitions between ideas and points. Too few transitions may make following the argument of the paper difficult; an overabundance of transition words may mean that the individual ideas are not sufficiently developed.

Commenting on a Paper

One of the basic assumptions underlying WANDAH's design was that students could use the system for peer interaction, a proven technique for improving writing. Using the commenting aid, students may read through each other's papers and make comments. The teacher may also use this aid to insert comments into a student's paper. Wherever the reviewer wants to comment, she or he simply presses the <INSERT> key. The screen opens and the reviewer just types in the comments, which appear in boldface and underlined. After the review session, the paper is saved on the disk along with the inserted comments. These may later be looked at by the original writer either on the screen or in a printed form; in the printed copy, the comments are inserted in the text indented, underlined, and single spaced.

Documentation

Although WANDAH presents students with copious on-screen prompts and descriptions, we also realize the need for written documentation of the system. WANDAH has a student manual, which includes the written tutorial, a troubleshooting guide, and explanations of the prewriting and revising aids.

The Development Process

No one should design a computer program without a clear understanding of what its eventual users want and expect it to do. Our design team therefore met several times with UCLA Writing Program lecturers and administrators. We wished to base our design on existing teaching practice, and we needed to know which writing aids and teaching techniques teachers would willingly delegate to a computer and which ones they wished to reserve for themselves. We did not intend to design sophisticated writing aids with no pedagogical value or with little chance of being used. Not surprisingly, we learned that all of our proposed writing aids had analogues in actual classroom practice and that none of them had unanimous support. This meant that our system design had to allow instructors to use those aids they thought important without requiring the use of them all.

Armed with a clearer sense of what writing teachers wanted and expected, we began the detailed design. The project director storyboarded WANDAH's main components and submitted them to the other members of the design team. The storyboards depicted what WANDAH's various components would look like on the screen and indicated how a user would move from one component to another. Each design team member reviewed the storyboards, contributed comments, and suggested changes. The storyboards were continually redrawn and expanded at this stage.

The Word Processing Writing Project originally planned to integrate computerized writing aids with an existing commercial word processor. We soon concluded, however, that that wouldn't work. No existing word processor had all the features we felt were essential. Furthermore, modifying an existing word processor would have required complex licensing agreements with the word processor's publisher and would probably have proved as difficult as designing our own from scratch. We therefore decided to design our own word processor, even though we recognized it was a monumental task, unanticipated in our original grant proposal to the Exxon Education Foundation. Nonetheless, it gave us the chance to design a truly integrated writing system, a system over which we would have total control.

We had not yet considered in which programming language or languages we should code WANDAH nor had we decided on which machine or machines it would run. We found choosing our target machine difficult early in the development process. The microcomputer industry had begun introducing a new generation of computers, machines that ran faster, had more memory, and incorporated more sophisticated keyboards and displays than the more established machines. So, rather than prematurely tie our design to any one machine, we postponed the choice. Instead, we continued the storyboard development and based our preliminary design upon those features we assumed the new machines most likely would incorporate. Our target machine, we decided, would need at least 128,000 bytes of memory, two disk drives, a keyboard that included many programmable function keys, and a screen that had upper- and lowercase, that could display 24 80-character lines, and that could display reverse video and other special visual effects. Several of the newer computers offered these features and more were expected to.

Choosing a programming language proved an easier matter. We needed a language that would let us design the program in pieces, that would let us make efficient use of the machine's memory, and that would let us postpone choosing our target machine as long as possible. UCSD Pascal, in fact, had been specifically designed to operate on a variety of machines. The language also possessed features that made the development of large programs practical.

Once we had chosen our programming language, we hired UCLA student coders. Even though we had not yet completed the system's design, some parts of the design had been specified, and programming of those parts could proceed while the design team finished their work on others. We knew that, in any case, programming considerations and new insights would probably lead us to modify our design repeatedly as the project continued. Our coders did their original development work on Apple II computers because the project had Apples available to it and the Apples supported UCSD Pascal. We hoped that we could transport our work to our eventual target machine without too much difficulty. We had judged correctly; although we encountered some minor difficulties, we did successfully transfer our work when we finally obtained our target machine.

It was at the preliminary stage that we made a tactical error. We had decided to code the word processor first since it would be our most complex and time-consuming task. The coders wrote small programs, each of which would implement a single feature of the word processor. We hoped that we would then be able to integrate them into a single program, but we underestimated how interconnected the word processor's individual functions were. The integration became nightmarishly complicated, and major parts of our original code had to be completely rewritten.

While we wrestled with the word processor coding, other phases of the design continued. The design team settled on a target machine, the newly released IBM PC. We also chose a development machine, a Sage II. Both machines supported UCSD Pascal and they could each read floppy disks prepared on the other. Using two different machines kept us honest—we wished to make sure that our design remained more or less independent of any one machine's peculiarities.

Meanwhile, our coders entered the design process. They were students, representative of our system's proposed audience, and they had definite opinions about what a writing aid should do. Their suggestions contributed significantly to WANDAH's design. Each suggestion, however, often meant a design change, and each design change meant a programming change, and each programming change made integrating the word processor components more difficult.

Finally, after much labor, we integrated enough of the word processor to begin our formative evaluation. We let several people outside the project use the partially completed word processor, noted their comments and difficulties, and spotted and corrected many bugs. Design changes continued, but we had now developed more fruitful techniques of incorporating them. The word processor programming accelerated, and we were able to assign some of our student programmers to WANDAH's revising aids.

WANDAH is now nearly complete. We are conducting the formative evaluation at UCLA, the University of Minnesota, the University of Washington, and the Punahou High School in Honolulu. We are looking not only at the effectiveness of the WANDAH system for improving writing but also at the dynamics of its classroom use. Following development and testing, we intend to make WANDAH available through a commercial publisher.

We believe that WANDAH will provide a rich arena for future research well beyond the expiration of the funded project. The usefulness of invisible writing as an unblocking aid, the effectiveness of the various organization programs, the importance of the special word processor—all are topics for exploration. Perhaps the most important research of all, however, will be on the impact of the system as an integrated whole on student writing.

References

Bereiter, C. 1979. Development in writing. In *Testing, teaching, and learning: Report of a conference on research on testing*, ed. R. Taylor and S. White. U.S. Department of Health, Education, and Welfare and National Institute of Education: 146–166.

Burns, H., and G. Culp. 1980. Stimulating invention in English composition through computer-assisted instruction. *Educational Technology* 20 (Aug.): 5–10.

Cohen, M. 1982. HOMER: A computer program looks at style. *Perspective* (Office of Academic Computing, University of California, Los Angeles) 6 (3).

Collier, R. 1983. The word processor and revision strategies. *College Composition and Communication* 34 (May): 149–155.

Daiute, C. 1983. The computer as stylus and audience. *College Composition and Communication* 34 (May): 134–145.

Elbow, P. 1973. *Writing without teachers.* New York: Oxford University Press.

Emig, J. 1971. *The composing processes of twelfth graders.* National Council of Teachers of English Research Report no. 13. Urbana, Ill.: NCTE.

Flower, L. 1981. *Problem solving strategies for writing.* New York: Harcourt.

Hayes, J., and L. Flower. 1979. Protocol analysis of writing process. Paper read at the Annual Meeting of the American Educational Research Association, San Francisco.

Kiefer, K. 1982. Report on a test of the Writer's Workbench at Colorado State University. Paper read at FIPSE Consulting Conference on Computers and University Writing Programs, Minneapolis.

Marcus, S. 1983. Real-time gadgets with feedback: Special effects in computer-assisted writing. *The Writing Instructor*, Summer.

Nancarrow, P. 1983. Integrating word processing into a freshman composition curriculum. Paper read at the Annual Meeting of the Modern Language Association, New York.

Schwartz, H. 1982. Monsters and mentors: Computer applications for humanistic education. *College English* 44 (Feb.): 141–152.

System Requirements

WANDAH runs on an IBM PC with at least 128K RAM and two disk drives.

Program Availability

WANDAH should be commercially available in the fall of 1984.

12 Wordsworth II: Process-Based CAI for College Composition Teachers

Cynthia L. Selfe
Michigan Technological University

Every now and again I sit back to contemplate the mythic proportions of my job. Like most college English teachers in this country, I am charged each year with a heroic (if not downright fantastic) task, a task that makes slaying the Hydra look like a piece of cake. I am expected to guide over 200 students—mathematics, business, chemistry, and engineering majors of all abilities—through that wickedly complex maze we call the writing process. Each semester, I must teach these students how to brainstorm, plan, and focus their topics before they begin to compose; how to write multiple and increasingly successful drafts of their papers; and how to ensure that their text conforms to conventions of grammar and style as they approach a final written product. And if there is one thing I have learned from these labors, it is that I have too many students and too little time to do this job well.

Wordsworth II, a cooperative venture of English teachers and computer scientists at Michigan Technological University, is a program of computer-assisted instruction that supplements the process-based teaching we do in our freshman composition sequence. It offers English teachers a sophisticated and interactive program of computer-assisted instruction that addresses all parts of the composing process from the initial planning of a topic through the polishing of a final paper. This CAI promises to lighten the burden of teachers by providing their students with tutorial help outside of regular classroom hours.

An Overview of Wordsworth II

Wordsworth II consists of eight, process-based modules that supplement classroom instruction in composition. Each module is focused on one

I would like to thank my colleagues Billie Wahlstrom, Bruce Petersen, Nancy Guinn, and Dickie Selfe for their help with this article and their work on Wordsworth II.

of eight writing assignments most commonly given in college composition classes: description, narration, classification, evaluation, persuasion, writing in personal journals, comparison and contrast, and writing about literature.

The Wordsworth II team has completed and begun to field test the first module on writing narratives. The remaining modules are being written and should be completed and field tested by the end of 1984. All the modules will follow a similar format; each will be divided into two programs, PLANNING and POLISHING, as shown in the figure below.

The PLANNING program of each module reviews for students the major lecture points associated with the assignment and then involves them in strategies they can employ before beginning to write a paper: brainstorming to generate or invent possible topic ideas, exploring and focusing potential topics through short journal entries or freewriting,

Writing a Narrative

PLANNING

Reviewing lecture points
Inventing potential topics
Focusing on topic
Organizing plot line
Considering audience

POLISHING

EARLY Draft

Identifying aim and purpose
Identifying audience
Identifying focus
Considering organization
Eliminating deadweight
Defining major strengths
Defining major weaknesses

MIDDLE Draft

Working with organization
Showing vs. telling
Focusing on a central theme
Creating effective introduction
Writing dialogue

LATER Draft

Considering transitions
Employing vivid verbs
Punctuating dialogue
Checking spelling

Prototype Module. Outline of the Wordsworth II prototype module, Writing a Narrative.

organizing plot lines, and constructing audience profiles. The POLISH-
ING program, divided into EARLY draft, MIDDLE draft, and LATER
draft branches, involves students in various strategies of revising, recast-
ing, or proofreading, depending on the type of draft they bring to
the computer. Students using this part of the program still do most
of their writing at home, coming to Wordsworth II only after they have
worked through the problems associated with each successive draft. The
POLISHING program helps students find their papers' strengths and
remaining weaknesses and plan a rewriting strategy.

How Wordsworth II Works

One of Wordsworth's most important functions is as a supplementary
instructional tool. We have not designed the program to take the place of
teachers or tutors; rather, we hope that it will assist these people in
getting across the important information about the processes involved in
writing and provide them relief from the more mechanical and repetitive
tasks involved in teaching writing. The PLANNING section of the narrative module, for example, begins with a review of lecture points on conflict, character, plot, detail, setting, and motivation. The points are
explained at several branching levels, each level involving its own examples and practice exercises. Thus, students can select the amount of
explanation and practice most appropriate for their own understanding
of the subject. A student confident about the narrative lesson can choose
only a brief reminder of each lecture point, while a confused student may
select several increasingly complete explanations of a particular point. In
the following conversation, taken from one first-year student's session
with Wordsworth II, two levels of explanation are provided:

```
Point #1: Show your audience the scene
you are writing about, don't just tell
the audience about it. You know, Shawn,
the special challenge in writing a
narration is to recreate the scene for
your reader. You have to bring the
situation to life by providing very
vivid, explicit details that document
what happened and how it happened. This
```

use of vivid examples to recreate a
scene is called <u>showing.</u> Obviously, it
involves much more than just <u>telling</u> a
story. Often sensory details help to
<u>show</u> what is happening-details of sight,
sound, smell, touch, and feel. Other
times, details about someone's thoughts
or feelings help you show what is going
on. The use of vivid verbs can also help
<u>show</u> what's happening.

Take a look at the following examples.

<u>Telling</u>

John fixed breakfast.

<u>Showing</u>

John stifled a yawn, shuffled to the
kitchen, opened the refrigerator, and
removed the ingredients for a hearty
breakfast. While reading the sports
page of the <u>Times</u>, he dumped a cup
of milk over a large bowl of stale
Fruit Loops and downed three cups of
lukewarm coffee. He was ready to
start the day.

Do you get the idea, Shawn, or do you
need some practice in distinguishing
showing from telling? Type <u>YES</u> if you
do; type <u>GO ON</u> if you do not.

YES

Okay, let me see if I can't clarify this
business for you by illustrating the

difference between <u>showing</u> and <u>telling</u>.
Read the two paragraphs below and choose
the one that <u>shows</u> you what is going on-
that recreates the situation for you.
When I flash this on the screen, *, type
in the number of the paragraph you've
chosen, and I'll tell you what I think.

(1) I didn't want to watch Dickie do
it, but I couldn't stop myself. He
clambered up the ragged, gray rock
face, grabbing on to the small,
fragrant juniper bushes to steady his
progress. Once, when he shifted his
feet, small showers of pebbles
cascaded down the cliff and onto the
piles of massive boulders below. When
he reached a narrow ledge fifty feet
above where I stood, he stopped,
turned, crouched slightly, and
launched himself into the air. By the
time he hit the water, I was a
nervous wreck.

(2) I didn't want to watch Dickie do
it, but I couldn't help myself. He
climbed the rock face, got to a
ledge and dove off into the water.

Now, Shawn, which paragraph <u>shows</u> you
what happened? Type in the number.

* #1

That's the ticket, Shawn! The first
paragraph recreates the situation using
some very specific details (juniper
bushes, narrow ledge, fifty feet) and
some vivid verbs (cascaded, crouched,

```
launched). The author of this paragraph
invited you to watch the action that was
happening, just as she had done
originally. She wanted to show you the
story, not tell it to you.
```

If Shawn had not been able to identify the correct response after three tries at recognizing the difference between showing and telling, Wordsworth II would send him to his teacher or tutor for help.

Although this lecture review is helpful, it does not illustrate what we think of as Wordsworth II's greatest strength as a teaching tool for composition programs—it makes students write. The programs ask students to compose directly on the computer keyboard at each phase of the writing process, from the initial steps of planning and idea generation to the final stages of proofreading and polishing. The narrative module, for instance, asks students to begin thinking about their papers by brainstorming ideas about potential topics and listing them on the screen; to type freewriting, or preliminary stream-of-consciousness explorations of a topic; to revise paragraphs; and to type in profiles of characters, plot lines, and audiences. The following excerpt shows how Wordsworth II helped one student, Therese, focus on a tentative narrative topic, explore that topic in five minutes of freewriting, and then build profiles of the characters she plans to use in the narrative:

```
    Okay, Therese, you've done short
journal writes on three topics that you
think might be suitable for your
narrative assignment-running away from
home, the time I tried to tip my baby
brother out of his crib and roll him
down the stairs, and the time Don Bliss
asked me out. With which of these topics
do you want to continue? It might be the
one you like best, the one about which
you have the most to say, or the one you
think will interest your audience the
most. When I type *, you write in the
topic you've chosen.

*THE TIME DON BLISS ASKED ME OUT
```

Therese, I think that's a great choice. But let's try a focused journal write on that topic to make sure. I want you to take five minutes to tell me the story by typing it in on my screen. Remember, this is a freewrite, so you don't have to worry about grammar and spelling.

I really want to know what the major events of your narrative are and how you feel about what happened. Because this is your second journal write on this topic, you can begin to remember some detail, choose some location in which to set your story, and think of the point or message you are trying to get across to your reader by telling this story. I hope my directions are clear. Onward!! Remember, no more than five minutes!

LIKE I SAID BEFORE, I GUESS I WANT TO TALK ABOUT THE TIME I THOUGHT DON BLISS ASKED ME OUT. THE PROBLEM WAS THAT HE WAS ASKING ME FOR A FRIEND BUT I THOUGHT HE WAS ASKING FOR HIMSELF. THIS HAPPENED AT CHARLEVOIS HIGH SCHOOL WHERE I WENT TO SCHOOL. I WAS ABOUT 16 AND SO WAS DON. HE WAS REALLY A HUNK BUT HE NEVER PAID TOO MUCH ATTENTION TO ME AND I WAS TOO SHY TO LET HIM KNOW HOW I FELT. I KEPT FANTASIZING ABOUT US BUT THAT'S AS FAR AS IT WENT UNTIL ONE DAY AFTER CLASS WHEN HE ASKED ME IF I WAS GOING TO THE GAME AND I SAID NO. OF COURSE I THOUGHT HE WANTED TO TAKE ME BUT HE WAS ASKING FOR A FRIEND. I WAS SO STUPID THAT WHEN I FOUND OUT THE TRUTH I WAS TOO EMBARRASSED TO LET ON WHAT I HAD THOUGHT. I WANT TO LET OTHER GIRLS KNOW

THAT THEY HAVE TO BE HONEST OR THEY'LL
END UP IN THE SAME SITUATION. ALSO MAYBE
I WANT TO TALK ABOUT HOW I THOUGHT DON
BLISS WAS SO GREAT UNTIL I LEARNED
BETTER. YOU CAN'T JUDGE A PERSON FROM
HIS LOOKS. HE HAS TO BE HONEST ABOUT HIS
FEELINGS TOO. IF EVERYONE WAS HONEST
DATING WOULDN'T BE SO HARD IN HIGH
SCHOOL.

Well, Therese, how many major
characters (very important characters)
do you plan to have in your narrative?
How many are really needed to get your
story across to the audience? Below, I
want you to list each of the major
characters you plan to use by name. I
also want you to write a paragraph or so
about each character. You can tell me
about things like their age,
personality, friends, hobbies, or
concerns.

In addition, you might try painting a
descriptive picture of these people. How
do they walk? Talk? Laugh? How do they
sit in class? What kind of car do they
drive? Remember, the more you write now
about these characters, the easier it
will be to write a first draft of your
story.

1. DON BLISS. THE SCHOOL HUNK, A JOCK.
SAT NEXT TO ME IN ECONOMICS BUT ONLY
TALKED TO PATTI FROBERG, SCHOOL FOX. HE
WAS TALLER THAN ME, LOTS OF MUSCLE ONLY
NOW I THINK A LOT OF IT WAS PROBABLY
FAT. HE HAD GREEN EYES, BLOND HAIR, AND
A SORRY GRADE POINT AVERAGE. HE DECIDED

TO GO TO MICHIGAN STATE JUST BECAUSE HE
WAS A FOOTBALL PLAYER. ALWAYS GOT As AND
Bs IN ALL HIS CLASSES EVEN THOUGH HE
SLEPT THROUGH MOST OF THEM. I WORKED
HARD EVERY NIGHT AND BECAUSE I DIDN'T
PLAY FOOTBALL THE TEACHERS DIDN'T EVEN
CARE. ONE DAY HE STOPPED ME AFTER CLASS
TO ASK ME IF I WAS GOING TO THE GAME
WITH LINCOLN HIGH SCHOOL. THAT WAS THE
START OF MY TROUBLE. I'LL WRITE ABOUT
THAT. I CAN STILL REMEMBER ALL THE GIRLS
THAT USED TO HANG AROUND HIS LOCKER
BETWEEN CLASSES. HE WALKED LIKE ALL THE
FOOTBALL PLAYERS AND ALWAYS LOOKED
AROUND TO SEE WHO WAS WATCHING. HE WAS
SO CONCEITED.

2. ME-THERESE OSTANEK. SKINNY AND SHORT,
BLONDISH HAIR TO MY SHOULDERS. POPULAR-
BUT NOT TOO MUCH IN HIGH SCHOOL. I LIKED
DON BUT I NEVER TOLD HIM. I HATED HIGH
SCHOOL AND DID BAD IN ALL MY CLASSES
EXCEPT FOR MATH WHERE MR. SHIRLEY GAVE
TESTS. I ALWAYS DID GOOD ON THOSE
BECAUSE I COULD DO ALL THE PROBLEMS AND
DON ALWAYS SAT THERE AND COPIED MY PAPER
OVER MY SHOULDER. I NEVER EVEN TOLD HIM
TO STOP. MY LAUGH IS NORMAL. I LIKE
PARTIES, READING, AND MOVIES. BUT I WANT
TO WRITE ABOUT ME IN HIGH SCHOOL AND HOW
DUMB I WAS BECAUSE I THOUGHT DON WAS
ASKING ME OUT ON A DATE. MAYBE I CAN SET
IT IN MATH CLASS WITH DON COPYING.

Okay, Therese, how many minor characters
(characters of lesser importance) do you
plan to have in your story? List them by
name and write one or two sentences
about their most important

characteristics. Try to stick to those things that have a direct bearing on the story you are going to relate.

1. PATTI FROBERG. I'VE ALREADY TALKED ABOUT HER. SHE WAS THE MOST POPULAR GIRL IN THE SCHOOL. SHE WENT OUT WITH LOTS OF GUYS-ALWAYS FOOTBALL PLAYERS OF COURSE. SHE HAD GREAT CLOTHES, RICH PARENTS, LOTS OF FRIENDS. SHE WAS A CHEERLEADER IN HER FRESHMAN YEAR BUT GOT KICKED OFF THE SQUAD FOR GRADES.

2. DICK SOLDOSKI. A FRIEND OF DON'S FROM ANOTHER SCHOOL. HE WAS THE OPPOSITE OF DON, SKINNY AS A BEAN, ACNE, A CREEP. OF COURSE HE WAS THE ONE I HAD TO GO OUT WITH. I NEVER HATED ANYONE SO MUCH. THE WHOLE THING WAS HORRIBLE AND I COULDN'T WAIT TO GO HOME.

Are all these characters strictly necessary to the conflict you have identified, Therese? Can you cut any of them out? Remember, you don't have to tell the story exactly as it happens. Sometimes it helps your narrative to combine two characters into one! I'll list each of the characters you have identified. After I write their name, you write a sentence telling why it is necessary to have them in your story. Hit the carriage return when you're done with each character.

Don Bliss: HE WAS THE ONE THAT I REALLY LIKED. HE HAS TO ASK ME OUT.

Me, Therese Ostanek: I AM NECESSARY. I'M

```
THE ONE WHO GETS CONFUSED AND
EMBARRASSED BY THE WHOLE THING. ME IN
HIGH SCHOOL.

Patti Froberg: I GUESS SHE'S NECESSARY.
I WANT TO SHOW HOW EVERY GIRL IN MY
SCHOOL WANTED TO GO WITH DON. SHE WAS
THE MOST POPULAR ONE. SHE CAN BE LIKE
ALL THE GIRLS COMBINED. MAYBE I CAN JUST
SHOW HOW SHE FLIRTS WITH DON AND TALKS
TO HIM IN CLASS. MAYBE THE LOCKER THING
WILL BE GOOD.
```

Although Wordsworth II cannot judge the quality of the students' responses, it can respond to the length or the number of such responses. If a student writes a journal entry that is less than two sentences, for example, Wordsworth II asks them to "write just a bit more for me." If students are asked to brainstorm a list of at least five ideas and only respond with three, Wordsworth II asks them to "think for a few more minutes and come up with at least two more ideas."

Because use of Wordsworth is voluntary for freshman English classes, it must encourage neophytes as well as more experienced computer users. We cannot allow students to be scared away from the instructional material because they fear computers. Thus, we have tried to write the Wordsworth II modules in a lively, engaging style and conversational tone. The modules avoid computer or composition jargon and complicated file manipulations. All a student has to do to work with Wordsworth II is insert two diskettes into numbered disk drives and press "R" to start the program.

We have also programmed Wordsworth II to provide students with written records of their computer sessions. This has proven to be an exceptionally popular feature with the students who have field tested the prototype module on narration. They appreciate the opportunity to take home the journal writings, plot lines, audience and character profiles that they have created in response to the program's promptings and the chance to use the material in writing drafts of papers. These records are also useful for teachers or tutors who are working with students on specific writing problems and researchers who want to see how ideas and concepts are developed through planning and successive drafts.

How Wordsworth II Fits into the Classroom

Currently, in experimental classes, Wordsworth II is used as a voluntary tutorial outside of class. A teacher may begin a unit on narration, for example, by lecturing on narrative techniques, discussing appropriate readings, or outlining a narrative writing assignment for students. The teacher may also give students the option of working with Wordsworth II as they develop and draft their narrative papers. Those students who choose to use Wordsworth II then come into our Language Laboratory at their own convenience.

Although they can access any part of the Narrative module, typically students start with PLANNING, which helps them generate and focus their narrative topic in a session that lasts between 45 minutes and an hour. They can then go home, compose one or more drafts of their paper, and come back to the computer to use POLISHING. Students who return with the first draft of their text can access the EARLY draft section of the Narrative module, which helps them evaluate their success in focusing and organizing their story and in working with the rhetorical constraints of aim and audience, again in a session lasting approximately an hour. Students then leave the computer, make revisions based on their experiences with Wordsworth II, and come back with second or third drafts of their narrative. At this time, they use the MIDDLE or LATE draft portions of the program to refine further their stories' organization and focus; create effective narrative scenes, introductions, and transitions; and check for punctuation and spelling conventions. Students can then make a final revision of their paper before they hand it in to their teachers. Not all students, of course, choose to use Wordsworth II so frequently for every paper they write. Students can choose when and how often to use the program for each assignment. Some employ the program only for planning; some bring only one draft of an assignment back for the computer tutorial.

As students work through the modules on narration, description, persuasion, etc., their teachers may choose to follow their progress. Teachers can at any time access Wordsworth II's files for a listing of students who have used particular units. These files will also identify the amount of time each individual has spent on a module or unit. In addition, teachers may ask students to bring in or hand in drafts that they have written with the computer's help or copies of the conversations they have had with Wordsworth II.

Although we have used Wordsworth II only on a limited, experimental basis, we have seen how the program can lighten the burden of composition teachers. Because their students use the Wordsworth II programs to review and practice the writing concepts and techniques that are covered in class, teachers of the experimental sections find themselves making fewer explanations of points already covered in class lectures. Moreover, because students who use Wordsworth II are guided through the revisions of at least three drafts, teachers do less personal conferencing with students who need direction in revising.

Why Wordsworth II Works

We believe that Wordsworth II is successful as a supplementary program of computer-assisted instruction in composition because it grows out of a collaboration between English teachers and software design specialists. Each of the Wordsworth II modules begins with a script written by an English teacher familiar with rhetorical theory and pedagogy. These scripts identify the content for the various assignments, designate multiple levels of explanation and practice, and define criteria for evaluating student performance. Software design specialists then translate these scripts into programs that will operate on the microcomputers to which our students have access. These specialists also observe students who field test the modules so that inappropriate presentations, ambiguous directions, and ineffective exercises can be eliminated.

Collaboration has taught us some very valuable lessons. We have learned, for example, that such ventures take time at every stage. Each script requires a month or two to write. And each hour that we spend writing these scripts must be stolen from precious preparation, research, or personal time. Because we use student programmers, the programming of a script is a time-consuming effort. Generally, our students work ten hours a week, but their schedule is often interrupted by Michigan Tech's rigorous academic pace. Between mid-terms, finals, and vacations, we are lucky to average five hours of programming a week on our project. Finally, field testing our modules requires a great deal of time. When, for example, we finished writing our first Wordsworth II script and our programmers had finished programming it, we *thought* we were done. The first group of students we turned loose on that original software showed us just how naïve we were. They found ways to sabotage the programs that we hadn't even imagined. They muddied the waters of the clearest directions, chose alternatives that didn't appear on the screen, and wanted to quit in the middle of a 30-minute program to grab a burger at the union. We now know that any software not thoroughly field tested on the population for which it was designed is still in the first draft stage.

Nevertheless, we believe that collaboration is the foundation for our success, and because the response from our students and our colleagues has been so positive whenever we have demonstrated or talked about Wordsworth II, we are encouraged to continue the cooperative efforts we have begun.

What Students Say about Wordsworth II

If the student reaction to our prototype module is any indication, our cooperative effort has provided an effective alternative to the simplistic fill-in-the-blank CAI programs. Our students find Wordsworth II to be "enjoyable" and "almost as much fun as a video game." Perhaps more importantly, however, they find it to be useful in their own writing efforts. As one student noted:

> A computer program for creating English papers is definitely helpful. The most difficult part of a paper is finding a good topic. Not many students know the procedure for discovering a topic. Furthermore, most students are too lazy to sit down and follow the procedure to the finish. With computers, however, all information necessary for writing a paper is right in front of your face on a screen. The computer explains the step-by-step procedure for writing a paper. The student can develop the paper as quickly as he can type the information into the computer. If you discover that the topic chosen is not specific enough or wrong, you can easily erase everything and begin from scratch.
>
> The computer is like a game. It encourages the student to write. The computer also breaks the monotony of scribbling down information on paper. Since it is a machine that doesn't run forever and many people are usually in line waiting to use it, the student is pushed to type something when asked a question by the computer, making free-writing faster and easier. For most students, it's very difficult just to sit in front of a computer without typing in something. But when someone sits down to write a paper, he can sit for hours without writing anything.

This comment is representative of the responses we received from the first-year students who used Wordsworth II. All of the students who field tested the prototype module agreed that it was a "valuable" teaching tool. Not one of them complained of having to work with a mechanical teacher of composition or of feeling frustrated when trying to undertake a task of creative writing at the prompting of a computer. In fact, some students suggested that it might be easier to write on the computer than in the classroom:

> I think this program will help people. I became very comfortable with it, especially when it kept calling me by my name. The program

took me step by step through the process of writing a narrative so I
could sit there and concentrate on my own work—not like in class.
Besides, it was patient. Computers can't yell at you like teachers do.

We suspect that many students enjoy working with Wordsworth II
because of the private nature of the user-computer interaction. In many
of our composition classes at Michigan Tech, we ask students to show
their writing to their peers in group critique sessions and to their teachers
in one-to-one conferences. When they use Wordsworth II, they are
free to experiment, try new techniques, take chances—all without human
witnesses.

Perhaps most importantly, however, students like the fact that
Wordsworth II makes them slow down their writing process and try
different strategies at different stages of their planning, drafting, and
revising efforts.

Writing the paper with Wordsworth took a long time, but it was
worth it. I learned a bunch of different things to do the next time I
try to write. It especially helped me with planning. I hadn't really
known that there was so much to do before you even started to
write. I wish I could have learned about this program in high school;
my writing would have been more descriptive and interesting.

Often we find that our students are apprehensive about writing because
they recognize how few skills and strategies they have mastered for
tackling any given composing task. Such students appreciate the opportunity the program gives them to learn and practice techniques that they
can add to their repertoire.

In general, our field test students have been quite comfortable with
Wordsworth II. In the open-ended descriptions of their experiences that
we ask them to write when they complete a module, they have given us
no indication that further use of the program might meet with resistance.
Until more modules are completed, however, a formal series of studies on
student response cannot be undertaken. And without such experiments,
many of our questions about student response must remain unanswered.
We can only wonder, for example, if the novelty of the programs is
responsible for the initial enthusiastic reception; if the CAI helps students
write better, more fluently, or with less anxiety; if the strategies provided
by the programs help students write better in other classes across the
university curriculum; or even if the software improves students' performance in composition classes.

What Teachers Think of Wordsworth

Although we have completed only the first module of Wordsworth II, we
have already begun to seek the advice and suggestions of our colleagues

in improving the program. During the last two years, we have talked about Wordsworth II to hundreds of English teachers in conference presentations, journal articles, and personal correspondence and have demonstrated the software to composition instructors from a number of schools. The tenor of our colleagues' response has been very positive. Like us, they know that English teachers are laboring under heavy workloads and in difficult classroom situations. They also recognize that computer-assisted instruction like Wordsworth II can help them reinforce a process-based approach to composition and handle some of the more mechanical teaching tasks to which they must now devote valuable time.

The next two years should see us increasing our use of Wordsworth II in our own department and in English departments at other universities that have volunteered to field test the material. During this field testing, we would like to explore much more thoroughly how teachers react to the Wordsworth II programs. As part of our studies, we would like to find out how teachers perceive our CAI, how often and in what ways they use the software, what they identify as its pedagogical strengths and weaknesses, what they think must be added to our series, and what they think should be deleted.

What We Have Learned

Creating Wordsworth II has been an exciting experiment for us. When we began, none of us had any experience in computer programming; none had ever attempted to write CAI; and none had any idea how much time, effort, and money such a program entailed. Two years have passed; we have learned a little about all these things, but they are the least of our lessons. Above all, we have learned that composition teachers and computer specialists, working as a team, can create valuable, process-based software for composition classrooms. We hope that this lesson will encourage other teams to design, implement, and evaluate CAI for courses that involve technical and business writing, writing about literature, journalistic writing, and creative writing and that such CAI will help teachers in their own heroic labors.

References

Bishop, R., et al. 1973. Adapting computer-assisted instruction to the non-programmer. University of Michigan. ERIC Document no. ED 081 231.

Burns, H., and G. Culp. 1980. Stimulating invention in English composition through computer-assisted instruction. *Educational Technology* 20 (Aug.): 5–10.

Schwartz, H. 1982. Monsters and mentors: Computer applications for humanistic education. *College English* 44 (Feb.): 141–52.

Wresch, W. 1982. Computers in English class: Finally beyond grammar and spelling drills. *College English* 44 (Sept.): 483–90.

System Requirements

The Wordsworth II modules are programmed in UCSD Pascal and run on a Terak 8512 microcomputer with a minimum memory of 56K RAM. A dual disk drive accepting eight-inch disks is required.

Program Availability

All inquiries about Wordsworth II should be addressed to Cynthia Selfe Humanities Department, Michigan Technological University, Houghton, Michigan 49931.

13 Toward the Design of a Flexible, Computer-Based Writing Environment

Christine M. Neuwirth
Carnegie-Mellon University

Computer text editing programs provide a set of general, low-level editing tools to anyone who works with text—copyeditors, typists, or writers. A typical text editing program allows a person to insert, erase, and move words, sentences, paragraphs, and even entire sections of a manuscript without the tedious copying and recopying forced by traditional technologies. By using a text editor, a person can carry out plans for revision easily.

Writers, however, do much more than carry out plans for revision. They must also produce those plans, a task that often involves all the components of the composing process. Writers unfamiliar with computer text editors might expect such programs to be similar to human editors and assist them with these components as well. Unlike human editors, however, computer text editors cannot help writers decide what to say, how to organize their ideas, or how to improve their style. Text editors provide general help with managing the structure of manuscripts, but not the content.

DRAFT: A Computer-Based Writing Environment

This chapter reports an effort to design and build a computer program, called DRAFT, that integrates conventional text-editing facilities with tools to help writers with invention, arrangement, and style. The goals of the computer program are to provide writers, teachers, and researchers with a flexible, integrated, and easily used system that can (1) guide writers during the process of composing, (2) aid teachers in diagnosing problems and fostering change in students' composing strategies, (3) allow researchers to record the evolving processes and products of writers as they perform under natural or experimental conditions, and (4) provide all these users with a screen-oriented text editor to help them carry out their activities.

A writer using DRAFT views a computer terminal display screen that is divided into two parts, called windows.[1] The two windows allow different "pages" of manuscripts, notes, or reference works to be spread out and perused at the same time. For example, a writer can compose an abstract for a manuscript in one window while viewing pages from the manuscript in the other.

When a writer starts DRAFT, the following menu appears on the screen.

```
                Welcome to DRAFT          Draft1


DRAFT is a structured writing
environment, designed to aid you during
the process of writing. The system
offers instruction and advice while you
compose an essay using a text editor.

Please choose one of the following items
from the menu. Type the number of your
choice. You do not need to press the
RETURN key.

   1. How to use DRAFT: introduction and
      tutorial.

   2. Use DRAFT to compose.

   3. Index to DRAFT.

   4. Exit DRAFT.


edit help back next prev top goto acc
mark ret zog disp user find info win
xchg
```

DRAFT uses menus to display options to users and to allow them to choose an option quickly and easily. The menus in DRAFT contain two sorts of options: local and global. Whereas local options vary from display to display, global options remain the same across displays. In the sample menu, the local options are listed by number in the center of the screen.[2]

Besides allowing the user to move to another frame of information, local options can perform other actions, some involving single operations, others many. For example, option 4 in the sample menu simply exits the program. Options in other frames provide for complex actions such as locating all the passives in a manuscript.[3] In general, local options can be thought of as providing choices that are useful in the context of a particular frame.

Global options, on the other hand, are useful on every frame. Some of DRAFT's most important global options are the following:

edit allows a user to add, delete, or change information.[4] Writers can use the option to compose manuscripts. Teachers or researchers can use this option to create or modify instructional frames. Student writers can use it to edit manuscripts, but they can also use it as teachers would—to create their own instructional frames.

help provides instruction at any time in using the program, including on-line tutorials and definitions of global options.

back replaces the frame currently displayed with the frame displayed previously. The back option is one option of several (next, prev, top, goto, acc, mark, ret, zog, and find) which allow users to move through the frames of information in a flexible way. Such flexibility is important for accommodating different writing styles. For example, writers vary in the order in which they pursue writing processes. Some writers generate a single idea, consider where that idea fits in a developing organizational framework, and then carefully write the idea in a polished form. Others generate many ideas, consider how to organize them, and then draft an essay. One way to accommodate such variety is to provide writers with options for moving easily from one frame to another, allowing writers to move freely between the parts of a manuscript and also allowing them to access instructional guides as they need them.[5]

next replaces the frame currently displayed with the next frame on the same hierarchical level in the network of frames. Just as "canary" and "robin" are at the same level in a hierarchy of "animals," each of the options in Figure 2-1 is at the same hierarchical level. If an author selects the first option (Introduction) and then, after looking at that frame, types "n" (for next), the information for the second option (Use DRAFT to compose) appears. Writers can use the "next" option to move through a series of local options easily.

mark places the current frame on a list of frames that the writer wishes to be able to return to quickly. This option is useful because writers do not always pursue all goals to the same level of completeness as they work. They often make mental notes to return later to work on something in more detail. The "mark" option, coupled with the "return" option, allows writers to interrupt a sequence of goals at any point—to return to a higher-level goal in the sequence, or to go back and develop an earlier goal in more detail.

return displays a list of frames the user has previously marked and allows the writer to move to any of them.

To illustrate how the program assists student writers, the following simulated display shows how the screen might appear to a student who has been using DRAFT to compose an essay. The sample depicts the outline of an essay the student has been composing. Each option leads to a section of the student's essay, except for the last option, where the minus sign indicates that the user has either chosen not to write a conclusion or has not yet written one.

```
Undergraduate Education                    UE1


Should CMU require students to buy
personal computers?

    1.   Introduction

    2.   Background of the problem

    3.   Criteria an effective solution
         must meet

    4.   Statement of the solution

    5.   The solution meets the criteria

    6.   Discussion and refutation of
         alternative solutions
```

```
7.- Conclusion


edit help back next prev top goto acc
mark ret zog disp user find info win
xchg
```

Suppose the student wishes to see the introductory section of her or his essay. The student will type a "1," which causes the outline frame to be replaced by the introduction frame.

```
Introduction                           UE2

The decision reached on this issue will
affect every student in the university.
It will have an impact on education,
research, campus life, recruitment of
new students, the national image of CMU,
and the type of student CMU is likely to
attract.

                        C. Comment



edit help back next prev top goto acc
mark ret zog disp user find info win
xchg
```

In addition to the text of the introduction, the notation "C comment" appears on the screen. It indicates that someone who has permission to read the manuscript has added a comment. The user can choose to look at the comment by typing a "C."

```
Comment                          comment32


  1. Jane Doe [Class member]

  2. John Doe [Class member]
```

```
3. Harry Fish [Instructor]


edit help back next prev top goto acc
mark ret zog disp user find info win
xchg
```

The display shows several comments, identified by author. The student can choose to look at any of these comments by typing the corresponding number. The next display shows the comment by the student's instructor.

```
Harry Fish                              comment33

   You have a good sense of how this
   issue is likely to affect every aspect
   of student life. I'd like to see you
   elaborate. How will the decision affect
   education? Research? Consider giving
   both a positive and negative effect.


edit help back next prev top goto acc
mark ret zog disp user find info win
xchg
```

The student may now choose to look at other comments, to review other sections of the essay, or to revise the introduction in one window while viewing the teacher's comments in the other.

Suppose that while revising, the student decides that she or he would like to look at some of DRAFT's heuristic guidelines. A user can access the guidelines either from the options on the initial menu or through the global "goto" option. The next display shows the heuristic guides for developing problem statements derived from Young, Becker, and Pike (1970).

```
Problem Statements                      problem1

   1. What is the problem?

   2. Are the components of the problem
      clearly dissonant or incompatible?
```

```
3. Are the two components reasonable?
   Are they capable of verification?

4. What is the unknown?

5. Is the unknown relevant to the
   problem?



edit help back next prev top goto acc
mark ret zog disp user find info win
xchg
```

If the student selects the first option, he or she will see the display below. From this frame, the student can choose to see a definition of the term *problem,* view a model answer to the question, enter a conventional computer-assisted tutorial to explore for an answer, compose a response, or move on to another question. If the user composes a response, it will be saved on a frame so that she or he can return to it or perhaps later incorporate it into a draft of an essay.

```
What is the problem?                problem2


                          D. Definition

                          E. Example

                          T. Tutorial

                          C. Compose



edit help back next prev top goto acc
mark ret zog disp user find info win
xchg
```

The last sample display depicts how a split screen appears when a student reviews such a response together with the draft of an essay.

Jane Doe   UE92

Professor Fish
76-100

        Should CMU Require Students to Buy
                Personal Computers?

  A few weeks ago, Carnegie-Mellon
University announced a decision that
startled many students: to develop
personal computers at

edit help back next prev top goto acc
mark ret zog disp user find info win
xchg

What is the problem?   scratch17

    The University's decition to develop
personal computers at CMU clashses with
my values. The decision will raise
students' tuition unecassarily. I value
the lowest possible educational cost.

                               D. Definition

                               E. Example

                               T. Tutorial

                               C. Compose

edit help back next prev top goto acc
mark ret zog disp user find info win
xchg

Design Philosophy: Flexibility

There are clear advantages to making a tool such as DRAFT as flexible as possible. Although we have learned a great deal about the composing process, we still have a great deal more to learn. If a program is flexible, it can not only allow us to learn more about writing, but it can also be adapted to reflect new ideas. With this approach, we can also take advantage of the system's flexibility to help us *discover* optimal methods. This section discusses some of the many instructional procedures DRAFT attempts to accommodate and issues in teaching composing through DRAFT.

Variety in Instructional Methods

Until recently, instruction in composition focused on providing students with writing tasks and giving them knowledge of results, usually by commenting on the written products. Feedback based on knowledge of results, however, is often ineffective (Haynes 1978; Wolter and Lamberg 1976).

There are three reasons why feedback can be ineffective. The first is time delay. Students benefit most when they receive feedback quickly. If a student writes a challenging essay over a period of several weeks, and the instructor returns the essay a week after receiving it, a full month can have elapsed before the student receives feedback on parts of the essay. Instructors have developed several strategies for dealing with the problem of time delay. Some instructors require students to turn in intermediate drafts. Others require short essays that students turn in every week. Still others use the classroom as a forum for discussing students' work in progress, often with peer evaluation. DRAFT's design is flexible enough to support any of these strategies. DRAFT provides facilities for formatting and printing intermediate drafts. The program also allows teachers and class members to view work in progress without a printed copy and to comment on it.

The second reason feedback can be ineffective is that students often cannot attribute a problem in the written product to the process that caused the problem. Writing is a creative, open-ended activity in which there is no one correct answer and many ways to reach an adequate one. In learning or teaching such an activity, identifying the process which led to an inadequate performance is extremely difficult—especially if all we have access to is the final product. As Harris (1983) suggests, verbal protocols can provide useful information about students' intermediate steps. DRAFT can serve a very similar function by keeping a detailed record of all student actions during composing. We are exploring alternatives for structuring these records in a flexible way so that they can be used easily by students, teachers, and experimenters.[6]

The final reason feedback can be ineffective is that students often cannot generate alternatives to their failed strategies. Teachers have developed different pedagogies for helping students with this task. For example, Coles's (1981) pedagogy involves the careful sequencing of tasks so that students can discover alternative writing strategies themselves. In his textbooks, he typically presents students with a writing task and asks them task-specific questions. In one assignment, he presents students who have just written on the topic of amateurism and professionalism with another student's paper on the same topic (Coles 1981, 28–31). The assignment is to "write a paper in which you try your best to level with this student as a writer in a way that you hope can help him." Some task-specific questions Coles poses are the following: "Judging from this paper, what would you say the writer of it understood the assignment to mean or involve? What does that understanding enable him to do as a writer? What benefits were there for him, in understanding the assignment this way? What liabilities?"

Another method for teaching students alternative strategies is offered by Young (1980) and others whose pedagogy involves developing descriptive and analytic systems of heuristic procedures, often in the form of questions. Typically the questions are task- or domain-independent, applicable to many different writing situations. In this pedagogy, students are presented with these systems and asked to apply them to a variety of writing tasks. One such system, applicable to the above example from Coles, is that of stock issues: What is the problem? What is the solution? What are the good and bad consequences of the solution? Students should instance the questions as follows: What is the problem (for this writer)? What is the solution (proposed by this writer)? What were the good consequences (of his or her solution)? What were the bad consequences?

DRAFT attempts to accommodate the variety found in the teaching of alternative strategies by allowing instructors to modify already existing guides and to create their own.

Issues in Teaching Composition

At least some of the differences in teaching approaches among composition teachers arise because of research questions that remain to be answered.[7] Designing DRAFT forced us to confront many of these questions directly. We are committed to a design that can help us explore them.

The first question concerns how much guidance to give students and when to give it. This question arose in considering how to structure DRAFT's heuristic guidelines. One approach was presented earlier—at any time, students can access any of a large set of guidelines. In this approach, all the guidelines are structured hierarchically. The first level provides minimal guidance. Selecting an option at the first level leads to a second level with more detailed guidance in the form of definitions, prose models, and tutorials. The principle underlying this approach is that students already familiar with the questions need only look at the first frame; students unfamiliar with the guidelines or those wishing a detailed review can easily access additional guidance. All students, however, can access the same set of guidelines.

In another approach, students with different levels of skill would access different sets of guidelines. In such an approach, maximal direction can be given to students who are just beginning. For example, the first frame for beginning students might present a single question together with definitions of crucial terms. Next, they would view a prose model and a discussion of how it answers the question. Finally, they would enter a tutorial to help them produce an answer to the question for a particular writing task. As students refined their skills, guidance could be reduced and students encouraged to think for themselves. Although not yet implemented, we are studying ways to automatically track students into appropriate levels. The first time students access a guide, they would be tested and then tracked on the basis of their performance. The following display depicts a prototype screen for automatic tracking. The student must take the test; what the student would see after the test would be based on his or her test performance.

```
Introduction                          Summary4

Definition    A summary is a comprehensive
              but usually brief
              recapitulation of previously
              stated ideas.

Significance  The ability to summarize is
              important for both readers
              and writers. Skilled readers
              use summaries to help them
              understand and remember
              texts. Skilled writers use
```

```
                    summaries both to present
                    other points of view with
                    cogency and to focus their
                    readers' attention on
                    important elements in their
                    own texts.

Skills              Writing good summaries
                    requires effort and
                    judgment. To produce an
                    adequate summary, you must
                    learn to identify and select
                    important elements in a
                    text, to infer relationships
                    between those elements, and
                    to infer points that are not
                    stated in the original text
                    and state them in your own
                    words.

Options

                    1. Test in summarization
                    skills


edit help back next prev top goto acc
mark ret zog disp user find info win
xchg
```

The second design question concerns what form the heuristic guidelines should take. The guidelines presented earlier are domain-independent, intended to apply to many different writing tasks. To use such general guidelines, students must learn what tasks they apply to and how to refine them for particular tasks. An alternative would be to prepare guidelines for specific tasks. Students would then need to learn to generalize from the specific guidelines to new tasks. Both skills, generalization and refinement, are crucial in developing writing skill. Both approaches merit further exploration.

The third question concerns how actively to intervene during the process of composing. The DRAFT system is essentially passive. Students choose when to look at guidelines and when to respond to them. It may turn out, however, that a system with more active intervention develops skill more efficiently. By structuring local and global options differently and monitoring students' actions, we might help students achieve expertise more rapidly.

The final question concerns when to impose stages in teaching the writing process. The DRAFT system attempts to accommodate writers who execute component processes in any order. For example, they can produce some prose, rearrange some part, compose a new section, go back and revise the first section, and so on. Some pedagogies, such as Elbow's (1973) freewriting techniques, require writers to produce prose quickly and without revising. Although DRAFT can accommodate freewriting exercises, its emphasis on heuristic guidelines hardly encourages them. When should students be asked or required to impose stages on their writing processes? By monitoring the ways students write, especially the time they spend in executing component processes, we can explore answers to this question.

Future Plans: Evaluating the System

Will DRAFT be able to accommodate and even enhance students' composing processes? Our evaluation of DRAFT will attempt to address this general question by studies designed to answer the following questions:

> Do students produce essays judged to be of better quality using the system than they produce using more traditional technologies such as paper and pencil or typewriters? In what ways is the system effective and why? In what ways is it ineffective and why?
>
> Do students learn from the system? If they produce better essays when using the system, do they continue to do so when they write without DRAFT?
>
> Do writers consider the heuristic guidelines adequate, or are there important procedures that cannot be expressed in this framework?
>
> Do experienced writers and student writers use the system differently? If so, are there better ways to structure the environment for students?

Further plans for developing the system are contingent on the results of these studies.

Conclusion

DRAFT attempts to help students attend to important aspects of the process of inquiry, from formulating and exploring a problem to communicating the results of an inquiry. Given our understanding of instruction and writing, however, the most important feature of such a program is flexibility. By varying DRAFT's features and testing the ways in which both skilled and unskilled writers use the resulting systems, we can perhaps find ways to extend and revise our understanding of both the composing process and how to teach it. Our instruction can only be as strong as the theoretical base on which it rests. Thus, DRAFT represents an attempt to design an instructional system that can, at the same time, help us refine our theories.

Notes

1. The following describes DRAFT as it is initially being implemented. The implementation uses ZOG, a rapid response, large network, menu selection system for user-machine communication (Robertson, McCracken and Newell 1981). Because the implementation allows systematic variation of many of DRAFT's features, modifications may result based on experimental evaluations. At present, DRAFT is available only at Carnegie-Mellon. However, if the approach proves worthwhile, it might be more widely available.

2. Since frames of information are linked to other frames and those frames are in turn linked to still others, local options organize information in a hierarchical network of frames.

3. Simple actions, such as moving to another frame and exiting, are available from the ZOG operating system. More complex actions, such as locating all the passives in a manuscript, must be programmed.

4. It is possible to prevent changes to frames by specifying that the frame is not to be altered or deleted.

5. Another way is to tailor the structure of the guides to different sorts of writers. Experience with DRAFT may help decide between these alternatives.

6. Having access to such information assumes that the student has used DRAFT to compose an essay rather than to type in an already written essay. I do not mean to imply, however, that using a computer program such as DRAFT, either to compose or just to type, is good procedure. Whether or not it is requires further research.

7. Even if these questions were answered, however, a flexible system would still be useful to accommodate different styles, of teachers and students alike.

References

Coles, W., Jr. 1981. *Composing II.* Rochelle Park, N.J.: Hayden.

Elbow, P. 1973. *Writing without teachers.* New York: Oxford University Press.

Harris, M. 1983. Modeling: A process method of teaching. *College English* 45 (Jan.): 74–84.

Haynes, E. 1978. Using research in preparing to teach writing. *English Journal* 67 (Jan.): 82–88.

Robertson, G., D. McCracken, and A. Newell. 1981. The ZOG approach to man-machine communication. *International Journal of Man-Machine Studies* 14: 461–88.

Wolter, D., and W. Lamberg. 1976. Research on the effect of feedback on writing: review and implications. University of Texas. ERIC Document no. 140 355.

Young, R. 1980. Arts, crafts, gifts, and knacks. *Visible Language* 14 (4): 341–50.

Young, R., A. Becker, and K. Pike. 1970. *Rhetoric: Discovery and change.* New York: Harcourt.

Bibliography

Annotated Bibliography

Bruce C. Appleby
Southern Illinois University

Anandam, Eisel, and Kotlar. 1980. Effectiveness of a computer-based feedback system for writing. *Journal of Computer-Based Instruction* 6 (May). Describes recordkeeping system and system for delivering instructor's comments to students.

Appleby, B. 1983. Computers and composition: An overview. *Focus* 9 (Spring). Overview of the field, including warnings on social, economic, and sexist implications of computer use.

Arms, V. 1982. The computer kids and composition. ERIC Document no. 217 489. Discusses use of CAI in technical writing course. Program has dictionary, format facilities, and memory for later revision.

Barth, R. 1979. ERIC/RCS report: An annotated bibliography of readings for the computer novice and the English teacher. *English Journal* 68 (Jan.). Designed for teachers and students, novices and advanced students. Covers philosophical issues, computer literacy, grading, software, research, and other topics.

Bean, J. 1983. Computerized word-processing as an aid to revision. *College Composition and Communication* 34 (May). Short article on how computer-assisted instruction can change revision process.

Bell, K. 1980. The computer and the English classroom. *English Journal* 69 (Dec.). Provides names of teachers to contact at schools involved. Compares Radio Shack TRS–80 Model I and the Apple II.

Bishop, Bishop, and Gardner. 1973. Adapting computer-assisted instruction to the non-programmer. ERIC Document no. 081 231. Program which scans journalistic essays for key words and emphasis.

Blundell, G. 1983. Personal computers in the eighties. *Byte* 8. Discusses why computer market will continue to expand in the 80s through use of personal computers in home, business, and educational environments.

Borque, J. 1983. Understanding and evaluating: The humanist as a computer specialist. *College English* 45 (Jan.). Argues for greater recognition of English professors who write software and establishes criteria for evaluating programs.

Bradley, V. 1982. Improving students' writing with microcomputers. *Language Arts* 59 (October). Aimed at elementary school teachers. Compares three word processing approaches in two studies (storytelling and sentence combining).

Bridwell, Nancarrow, and Ross. 1984. The writing process and the writing machine: Current research on word processors relevant to the teaching of composition. In *New directions in composition research,* ed. Beach and Bridwell. New York: Guilford Press. Covers current programs and research in college composition and implications for the future.

Burns, H. 1979. Stimulating rhetorical revision in English composition through computer-assisted instruction. ERIC Document no. 188 245. Describes an experiment with freshman composition classes. Positive findings in terms of number, sophistication, and refinement of ideas.

————. 1980. A writer's tool: Computing as a mode of inventing. ERIC Document no. 193 693. Provides a sample computer-student interaction on Theodore Dreiser. Interesting for literary-type skeptics.

Caldwell, R. 1980. Guidelines for developing basic skill instructional materials for use with microcomputer technology. *Educational Technology* 20 (Oct.). Designed for software writers. Offers advice for writing effective programs that allow user control and employ graphics, color, reinforcement, etc.

Cherry, L. 1982. Writing tools. *IEEE Transactions on Communications* 30 (Jan.). Describes a series of programs designed to improve writing by analyzing readability, sentence length, editing, spelling, punctuation, etc. Aimed at business uses.

Collier, R. 1982. The effect of computer-based text editors on the revision strategies of inexperienced writers. ERIC Document no. 211 998. Discusses experiment and reports positive findings (increase in number and complexity of revision operations) and negative ones (no overall quality change). Notes problems to be solved.

————. 1983. The word processor and revision strategies. *College Composition and Communication* 34 (May). Reports on the effects of word processing on the revision strategies of four writers; changes tended to involve lower-level features with few major changes in the texts.

Connell and Humes. 1981. Using microcomputers for composition instruction. ERIC Document no. 203 872.

Courter, G. 1981. Word machines for word people. *Publisher's Weekly,* Feb. 13. An author's account of how a word processor made her task easier and the final product better.

Daiute, C. 1983. The computer as stylus and audience. *College Composition and Communication* 34 (May). Discusses composition theory in the light of computer feedback. Emphasizes physical and psychological constraints and processes.

Epes, Kirkpatrick, and Southwell. 1979. The COMP-LAB approach: An experimental basic writing course. *Journal of Basic Writing* 2. A detailed description of a basic writing course using CAI. Includes both the classroom and the laboratory components. Emphasis on editing.

Estes, T. 1983. A commentary on *Reading and understanding: Teaching from the perspective of artificial intelligence. The Reading Teacher* 36. Reviews this Roger Schank book, pointing out the inadequacies of the writer's model of the computer as compared with the human mind. Cites implications for teaching children to read.

Fisher, G. 1983. Word processing—Will it make kids love to write? *Instructor,* Feb. An enthusiastic article in favor of word processors in schools. Briefly explains the process, the advantages, and some stumbling blocks.

Gould, J. 1981. Composing letters with computer-based text editors. *Human Factors* 23 (5). Reports how mature writers took longer in their writing when using text editors. Discusses "fun factor" of using computers.

Halpern, J. 1982. Effects of dictation/word processing systems on teaching writing. ERIC Document no. 215 357. Lists the challenges to teachers resulting from technological changes. Suggests how these challenges can be met in the classroom.

Hennings, D. 1981. Using computer technology to teach English composition. *The Education Digest,* April. Briefly points out some advantages and misconceptions in using CAI for elementary school composition.

Hiller, Marcotte, and Martin. 1975. Opinionation, vagueness, and specificity-distinction: Essay traits measured by computer. *American Educational Research Journal* 6. Early study done on computer grading of compositions by searching for key words that indicate vagueness, opinionation, etc. Discusses the problems raised.

Horodowich, P. 1981. Developing stylistic awareness on the computer: A tagmemic approach. ERIC Document no. 198 530. Describes program that helps students recognize clause structures.

Jaycox, K. 1979. Ware, oh ware, might the English class go? *Illinois English Bulletin* 66 (Winter). Discusses why humanists need to get involved in use of computers in teaching and the uses of computers in literature instruction.

———. 1979. Computer applications in the teaching of English. ERIC Document no. 183 196. Aimed at present and future English teachers. Discusses methodology in language, literature, and composition and how CAI can augment it.

Kiefer and Smith. 1983. Textual analysis with computers: Tests of Bell Laboratories' computer software. *Research in the Teaching of English* 17 (Oct.). Urges the use of Writer's Workbench for freshman composition students. Reports research on teaching editing skills and on affective changes.

Klieman and Humphrey. 1982. Word processing in the classroom. *Compute* 22 (March).

Kreiter and Kurylo. 1983. Computers and composition. *The Writing Instructor* 2 (Summer).

Lahey, G. 1979. The effect of instructional presentation sequence on student performance in computer-based instruction. ERIC Document no. 175 453. A study to determine whether sequence (e.g., rule-examples-practice vs. examples-rule-practice) results in differences in performance. No significant differences found. Concludes that learner control may have advantages.

Lawler, R. 1982. One child's learning: Introducing writing with a computer. ERIC Document no. 208 415. A case study of one child's introduction to computer composition.

Leibowicz, J. 1982. CAI in English. *English Education* 14 (Dec.). Provides a good overview of the state of CAI, including drill and practice, tutorial, dialogue, and text analysis and editing systems.

Macdonald, Frase, Gingrich, and Keenan. 1982. The Writer's Workbench: Computer aids for text analysis. *IEEE Transactions on Communications* 30 (Jan.). Describes a system incorporating programs discussed in Cherry's "Writing Tools" (see above). Programs will proofread, comment on style, provide reference information.

Magarell, J. 1983. How faculty members use microcomputers. *The Chronicle of Higher Education*, March 30. A short breakdown of different uses faculty members have for their computers.

Marcus, S. 1982. Compupoem: A computer-assisted writing activity. *English Journal* (Feb.): 96–99. Composing a poem as a computer game, with conclusions about the advantages and limitations of the technique.

Marcus and Blau. 1983. Not seeing is relieving: Invisible writing with computers. *Educational Technology* 11 (April).

Mullins, C. 1982. Why a word processor? *The Writer* 95 (8). Compares dedicated word processors and personal computers. Personal paean to the wonders of the machines for writers.

Nold, E. 1975. Fear and trembling: The humanist approaches the computer. *College Composition and Communication* 26 (Oct.). Attempts to debunk humanist fears about CAI by providing examples of creative, stimulating programs. Urges English teachers to get involved.

Page, E. 1968. The use of the computer in analyzing student essays. *International Review of Education* 14. Classic early study in the field. Raises philosophical questions and practical considerations in an enthusiastic endorsement of this alternative method of grading.

Paul and Payne. 1983. Computer-assisted instruction: Teaching and learning from basic writers. *The Writing Instructor* 2 (Summer).

Robertson, McCracken, and Newell. 1981. The ZOG approach to man-machine communication. *International Journal of Man-Machine Studies* 14. A discussion of ZOG, a system designed for communication between people and computers. Aimed at the computer specialist.

Rubin, A. 1982. The computer confronts language arts: Cans and shoulds for education. In *Classroom computers and cognitive science*, ed. Wilkinson. New York: Academic Press. Argues that programs should move towards a more sophisticated view of language.

Schwartz, H. 1982. A computer program for invention and feedback. ERIC Document no. 214 177. Describes SEEN, a program to assist character analysis in literature. Concludes that the invention aspect is highly beneficial, the feedback still clumsy.

———. 1982. Monsters and mentors: Computer applications for humanistic education. *College English* 44 (Feb.). Discusses different types of programs (text feedback, drill and practice, simulations, tutorials). Provides sources for obtaining software and criteria for choosing.

Schwartz, M. 1982. Computers and the teaching of writing. *Educational Technology* 22 (Nov.). Asserts the advantages of CAI in the writing process— notably how the greater ease of recopying aids the revision process.

Selfe and Wahlstrom. 1983. The benevolent beast: Computer-assisted instruction for teaching writing. *The Writing Instructor* 2 (Summer). Discusses Wordsworth II, a program designed for various assignments including narration, persuasion, etc.

Southwell, M. 1983. Computer-assisted instruction in composition at York College/CUNY: Composition for basic writing students. *The Writing Instructor* 2 (Summer). Discusses the use of computers for grammar drill and practice in remedial writing programs.

Wall and Taylor. 1982. Using interactive computer programs in teaching higher conceptual skills: An approach to instruction in writing. *Educational Technology* 22 (Feb.). Describes a CAI model for teaching narrative writing and a study involving mathematics instruction of handicapped children.

Wilson, K. 1981. English teachers: Key to computer literacy. *English Journal* 70 (Sept.). Encourages English teachers as those most adept at communications skills, to become computer literate.

Wolter and Lamberg. 1977. Research on the effect of feedback on writing: Review and implications. ERIC Document no. 140 355. Categorizes feedback as abstract or specific; positive, negative, or corrective; and task related or unrelated. Suggests that selective task-related feedback from peers may be the most effective.

Wresch, W. 1982. Computers in English class: Finally beyond grammar and drills. *College English* 44 (Sept.). Discusses tutorial and dialogue software, pointing out the advances made since the linear drill programs like PLATO.

———. 1982. Prewriting, writing, and editing by computer. ERIC Document no. 213 045. Describes four programs: one for prewriting, one showing how prewriting information can be structured in an essay, and two for editing.

———. 1983. Computer essay generation. *The Computing Teacher* 10 (March). Describes a prewriting program using various rhetorical approaches.

———. 1983. Computers and composition: An update. *College English* 45 (Dec.). Description of wide variety of programs being used around the country. Warns of potential and actual misuses.

Glossary of Computer Terms

AI Artificial intelligence. A branch of computer science concerned with finding how computers can be programmed to do the things that people do. Often interested in problem solving, vision, etc. Some researchers are exploring language.

BASIC Acronym for Beginner's All-purpose Symbolic Instruction Code. A programming language usually found on microcomputers.

Bit Binary digit. A single switch inside the computer which is capable only of holding one binary digit (1 or 0).

Byte A group of bits, usually 8. It takes one byte to represent a letter of the English alphabet. Therefore, only when bytes are present in the thousands is there sufficient memory within the computer to hold things like essays.

CAI Computer-assisted instruction.

CBE Computer-based education.

Computer language A series of short commands understandable to a computer. This may be a set of words as small as 25. Examples of languages are BASIC, Pascal, and Fortran. By and large, computers will not understand commands not related to a specific computer language.

Concatenate A computer term for joining two "strings," or series of letters, into one string. See also **String**.

CP/M An operating system used on many microcomputers. Once thought to be the standard operating system, but others have proven more popular. See also **Operating system**.

Disk drives Devices that allow programs and other forms of computer information to be stored permanently. Typically, a computer will transfer information from its memory to a disk drive so that the information can be retained after the computer starts work on another program or is turned off.

DOS Disk Operating System, the system used on most Apple computers. See also **Operating system**.

Editor A program that allows a computer user to change (edit) the contents of the computer's memory.

File Information which has been magnetically stored as a single unit. If a chapter from a novel were stored on a floppy disk, it would be called a "file" by the computer.

Floppy disk A circular sheet of plastic coated with iron oxide. Computers use floppy disks to store magnetically any of the information in a computer's own memory. Allows information to be stored for later use.

Hardware The computer itself and any other devices plugged into it, such as disk drives. See also **Software**.

K The abbreviation for kilo or 1000. Usually used to tell how many bytes or storage locations the computer has in its memory. 64K means a computer has 64,000 storage locations available for information.

Load The process of transferring information from secondary memory to the computer's internal memory (RAM). Having the computer transfer an essay from a floppy disk to the computer's main memory is an example of loading. See also **RAM**.

Mainframe computer The largest-size computer. It may have a central processor the size of a file cabinet, with millions of bytes of internal memory, plus the ability to process many programs at once.

Memory The place where information is stored in a computer. Memory size varies considerably from one type of computer to another. A microcomputer usually has 64,000 locations (64K), but larger computers may have millions of locations.

Microcomputer Any computer so small that its entire central processor is contained on a single silicon chip.

Minicomputer A computer with a central processor that can fit onto one electronic circuit board. Such computers normally have large internal memories (usually over a million bytes) and often can be used by more than one person at a time.

Operating system A program that controls the transfer of information on and off secondary memory and coordinates the internal operation of the machine.

Program A series of instructions to a computer. See also **Software**.

RAM Random access memory. Simply the place inside a computer where information is stored. Every time you press a key on the computer's keyboard, that letter is entered into the computer's memory or RAM.

ROM Read-only memory. Information that has been put into the computer at the time of manufacture. The contents of this memory is used by the computer to understand computer languages.

Save Since the computer's internal memory is very temporary, any contents of that memory that you might want to preserve need to be transferred to secondary memory for permanent storage. That transfer process is called "saving."

Secondary memory Any means of taking information out of the computer's main memory and storing it permanently outside the machine. A disk drive is an example of secondary memory.

Software Any computer program. Called "software" because programs are easy to change ("soft"), whereas the machine itself is hard to modify. See also **Hardware**.

String A series of characters typed into a computer. Computers see text not as words or sentences, but as a series of individual characters which can be joined or broken up in many ways.

Text editor A computer program that lets a programmer modify any input to a computer. Usually used to change computer programs. Later adopted for use with writing projects.

UNIX An operating system created by Bell Laboratories. See also **Operating system.**

Window The part of computer memory that may be displayed on the screen. Some programs allow users to see two separate parts of memory at one time. This allows the user to see both the beginning and the end of a long text, for example.

Contributors

Bruce C. Appleby is Director of Composition Programs at Southern Illinois University in Carbondale and has published in *English Journal, College Composition and Communication,* and numerous other publications on topics ranging from sexism in language to computers and composition. Past President of the Illinois Association of Teachers of English, Dr. Appleby is on the executive committee of the Conference on English Education and the Board of Directors of the Adolescent Literature Assembly of NCTE.

Lillian S. Bridwell is Associate Professor of English at the University of Minnesota. She has spoken and written extensively about revision, assessment, and computers in composition instruction. She is author (with Donald Ross and Paula Reed Nancarrow) of *Word Processors and the Writing Process: An Annotated Bibliography* and editor of *New Directions in Composing Research.* She is at work with Don Ross on two manuscripts on the theoretical implications of computers for writing.

Hugh Burns, a Major in the United States Air Force, directs the research program investigating how artificial intelligence tools and techniques can enhance computer-assisted instruction for the Department of Defense. He is assigned to the Air Force Human Resources Laboratory, Lowry AFB, CO. and has been an Associate Professor of English at the USAF Academy. He is best known for his research in computer-assisted instruction in English, for his three invention software packages, and for his publications on instructional computing in the humanities and social sciences. He is a member of the Executive Committee for the Conference on College Composition and Communication.

Michael E. Cohen, A Software Consultant for the UCLA Writing Programs, designs, implements, and evaluates instructional and administrative software. He has published and presented papers on computers and composition instruction and was a principal programmer for WANDAH—Writing-Aid AND Author's Helper, an integrated word processor and writer's aid package.

Colette Daiute, Assistant Professor of Education at Harvard University, was a 1980 recipient of NCTE's Promising Researcher in English Education Award. She has lectured and published widely on the computer in the writing process and has developed computer software. She has served as a consultant for the Children's Television Workshop and other organizations, and sits on the review board of the *Journal of Educational Psychology.* Her new book, *Learning to Write With (and Without) Computers,* will be published by Addison-Wesley in 1984.

Kathleen Kiefer, Associate Professor of English at Colorado State University, has written and presented papers on the application of computers to composition instruction and on the Writer's Workbench programs in particular. Her research interests also include basic writing and applied linguistics. She is author of *Making Writing Work: Effective Paragraphs* and *Thinking, Reading, Writing*. With Cynthia L. Selfe, she is coeditor of the quarterly newsletter *Computers and Composition.*

Richard A. Lanham was educated at Yale, taught briefly at Dartmouth, and since 1965 has been at UCLA, where he is Professor of English and Executive Director of the UCLA Writing Programs. He is the author of *Style: An Anti-Textbook, The Motives of Eloquence, Analyzing Prose,* and other books.

Stephen Marcus is Associate Director of the South Coast Writing Project at the University of California, Santa Barbara, where he is responsible for program design and evaluation and inservice training in computer literacy for English and language arts faculty. He has published articles on computer-assisted instruction in numerous journals and serves on the editorial and advisory boards of several journals including *Language Arts* and *Research in the Teaching of English.* He has developed software for the study and writing of poetry.

Christine M. Neuwirth is an instructor in the Department of English at Carnegie-Mellon University, where she teaches a graduate course in Computers and Rhetorical Studies, and a research associate in Carnegie-Mellon's Communication Design Center, where she directs the Writing Center. Her dissertation research involves the development of a computer program that will tutor students in writing sentences that satisfy multiple goals.

Dawn Rodrigues is Director of the Writing Lab and Assistant Director of Freshman Writing in the Department of English at New Mexico State University in Las Cruces. She has presented papers and published several articles on computer-based instruction.

Raymond J. Rodrigues, Professor and Department Head of Curriculum and Instruction and Director of the Teacher Education Program at New Mexico State University in Las Cruces, is on the Executive Committee of the NCTE Conference on English Education. He is the author of over forty articles on English teaching, computers in composition, and multicultural education, as well as coauthor of seven literature anthologies, *A Guidebook for Teaching Literature,* and *Mainstreaming the Non-English Speaking Student.*

Donald Ross is Professor of English and Co-Director of the Composition Program at the University of Minnesota. He was largely responsible for developing that university's series of junior-senior writing courses in the disciplines from the arts to engineering. With Professor Lillian Bridwell, he is co-principal investigator on a project to study the effects of computers on undergraduates and their teachers. Aside from publications emerging from that project, he is the author of several articles on the computer-aided analysis of literary works.

Helen J. Schwartz is Associate Professor at Oakland University, Rochester, Michigan. She has programmed computer software (SEEN for critical inquiry and ORGANIZE for prewriting) and has published essays on using computers in literature and writing instruction. She has also lectured widely on campuses and at conferences on computers and communication. Her text, *Interactive Writing,* using word processing in the teaching of composition, will be published by Holt, Rinehart and Winston in 1984.

Cynthia L. Selfe is an Assistant Professor of rhetoric and composition in the Humanities Department of Michigan Technological University. Her research interests include the writing process, writing and reading connections, and the use of computers in writing programs. She has published in such journals as *Research in the Teaching of English, College Composition and Communication,* and *The Writing Teacher,* and currently coedits *Computers and Composition* with Kate Kiefer.

Charles R. Smith is Associate Professor of English at Colorado State University. He has coauthored articles on computers in writing instruction and the Writer's Workbench programs at Colorado State in particular.

Michael G. Southwell teaches in the English Department at York College/ CUNY. Working closely with Mary Epes and Carolyn Kirkpatrick, he has administered several funded projects to create, evaluate, and disseminate a laboratory-centered basic writing course, has authored a successful basic writing workbook, *The COMP-LAB Exercises,* and has investigated the kinds of writing problems manifested by developmental students. For the last several years, he has been working on applications of computers to writing instruction. In this connection, he has made many presentations at professional organizations, has published a number of articles, and has consulted widely. He is a member of the Committee on Computers of the CCCC.

William Wresch teaches English and computer science at the University of Wisconsin Center–Marinette County. He was a 1982–83 recipient of an Apple Education Foundation grant to support the creation of a program to teach composition skills via computer. He has published and given papers on reading and writing connections and on computers in writing instruction.

Ruth Von Blum is Project Director of the Word Processor Writing Project at UCLA. She has been the recipient of several grants and has published widely in the fields of botany and computers in education. She serves on the editorial board of *Computers, Reading, and Language Arts.*